Thrice Trumpeted Truths

CLEARLY

spoken

3

times

J. Mark Holland

WestBow

PRESS

A DIVISION OF THOMAS NELSON

All Scripture quotations, unless otherwise indicated, are taken from the Holy Bible, King James Version (KJV).

WestBow Press books may be ordered through booksellers or by contacting:

WestBow Press
A Division of Thomas Nelson
1663 Liberty Drive
Bloomington, IN 47403
www.westbowpress.com
1-(866) 928-1240

ISBN: 978-1-4497-7401-1 (sc)
ISBN: 978-1-4497-7402-8 (hc)
ISBN: 978-1-4497-7400-4 (e)

Library of Congress Control Number: 2012920968

Printed in the United States of America

WestBow Press rev. date: 11/16/2012

jmh@3-truths.com

Contents

Preface

"Lets look for some threes (triples) in the Bible," I announced to our senior saints study group of about 30. But no excited looks! So what to do? I put my "life on the line" and began with Genesis 1. Then *eureka*!! A *triple* set of triples. We were on a roll. Maybe we can survive three sessions—possibly four. However, the path of discovery was amazing. It became an adventuresome six month journey.

We didn't find any hidden messages. We didn't look for any. What we found were awesome, uniquely described *thrice trumpeted truths* that proclaim many of the key doctrines of Scripture.

It was almost as though secrets were being discovered. Not secret new truths, but an unveiling of unique display patterns. Personally, I was moved to tears by some triples I had never noticed or heard mentioned—such as nine sets in John 18 & 19. They are *awesome*! These must be shared!

Having taught Bible courses, Bible classes, and Sunday school for more than 40 years and considering myself somewhat knowledgeable of the Scriptures, I felt confident that we could find some *thrice trumpeted truths*, but little did I realize that there are hundreds of such sets. Some sources claim that there are hidden codes in biblical numbers, but this was not our interest.

Class members became intrigued and began to identify triples from their own studies. We found so many that we had to end our search before looking at the Prophets, the Epistles, or the Psalms.[1] Might we find some in Revelation?[2]

It was amazing to see triples not simply as a repeated literary structure, but also as affirmations of key scriptural truths and evidence that God's inspired writers **"spake as they were moved by the Holy Spirit."**[3]

For example, it was captivating to find in the concluding book of the Old Testament that Malachi referenced the *truth* of the Messiah's coming three times (Malachi 3:1; 4:2; 4:5, 6). Then another prophetic truth *trumpeted*

---

[1] Someone found eleven sets of triples in First John. None of these are included in this study. (My conjecture: there are probably 12, a multiple of 3).

[2] Can you find *seven* sets in Revelation, chapter one?

[3] 2 Peter 1:21

thrice in the final chapter of Revelation: "**I come quickly**" **Revelation 22:7, 12, 20**. A *triple* concludes the final chapter of Revelation!

Are such repeats necessary? What about Elihu's indictment? He expressed an insight into human nature when he stated: "**For God speaketh once, yea twice, yet man perceiveth it not**" **(Job 33:14)**. Evidently a third *trumpeting* is needed.[4]

I dedicate this study to the memory and recognition of many pastors, Bible teachers and authors—past and present, that have faithfully taught the Word throughout my life. And now to each current student of the Bible, my prayer is that this study will spark greater interest as you "search the Scriptures" for *truths* in God's revelation.

Also, to any pastor, teacher, or group leader who needs some three point principles—more than 100 triples are identified in this book.

Note: We looked at triples in the King James Version[5] of the Bible. The KJV was chosen for at least three reasons:

- It is the most common English version available,
- It attempts to be a more literal translation, not simply a dynamic equivalent[6] that often loses some word or phrase nuances of the original languages.
- It does not require copyright permission or royalties to be quoted at length.

Personal Note: When writing, the rule is to always begin with an outline so you know where you are going. There was no outline. We didn't know what we were going to find. No books on the topic seemed evident. So, the only source was the Scripture itself. There was no intent to publish anything. However as the triples began to unfold, my thought: "This must be shared; it is awesome!"

Where to stop remained the question. The reality: we have not included four major sections of our findings: *The Names of God, The Tabernacle, The Feasts of the Lord,* and *Jesus visits to Jerusalem.*

(Sequel? Possibly! See: http://www.3-truths.com).

---

[4]   See: Brian Backman, *Thinking in Threes: The Power of Three in Writing,* Cottonwood Press, ISBN: 1-877673-67-6

[5]   We compared many passages with the NKJV and found no discrepancies.

[6]   Dynamic Equivalence is designed for readability and sentence flow—not for word equivalence.

Part One
Amazing

Section I
Why Three?

Curiosity! My curiosity was ignited by numerous multiple repeats in the Scriptures, especially in Genesis 6, 7, 8 (see *Appendix A*). The list is uniquely amazing.

Teaching the same senior adult class for nearly 30 years requires some new topics. Our adventure began with a question: "Since there are some repeats in the Scriptures, are there any significant, uniquely stated *triple* repeats?"

CHALLENGE

Let's find some!

We were convinced that finding *triply* repeated *truths* was not going to be simple. We did not find any specific books or other written resources to guide our search. We knew there were three crosses, three days, three gifts, Moses had three major encounters with God, and a few others.

I tried to involve the group. "Let's try to find some *threes* or *triples* in the Bible." That was a simple challenge. I expected two or three people to find one but I also ventured out on my own. Where to start? Why not Genesis? So I did. I already knew that the Hebrew word "create" (*bara*) was used, stating that God created **three** specific realms: the first *bara* is in verse one: "In the beginning, God created *[bara]* the heaven and the earth."

Then a "wow." Here was a triple.

► *beginning*—time.

► *heaven*—space.

► *earth*—matter.

Okay, good start. This was a *triple, triple* realization:

► **Time** for us has three components: past, present, future.

► **Space** has three dimensions: length, width, height.

► **Matter** consists of atoms: proton, neutron, electron.

Were we on a roll? For me the discovery of triples in God's Word became an amazing adventurous journey. Like Abraham, I didn't know where we were going or what we might find. What we found were *thrice trumpeted truths* that identify many of the key doctrines of Scripture.

It was almost as though secrets were being uncovered. Not secret new truths, but an unveiling of unique display patterns. The challenge as our study proceeded was not to simply find a truth and then find two more references to it, but rather to find a unique statement concerning a truth and then find *two* and *only two* more *"same"* statements in Scripture. That unique *triple* became another *thrice trumpeted truth*.

The question, "Why three?" became the key for our entire adventure. After all, if God says it once, shouldn't that be *sufficient?* To say something twice makes it *definite*. However, if God states a specific truth *three* times, that is evident that He wants to make *certain* that we both hear and heed what is said. Job's friend, Elihu, with insight into human nature stated: **"For God speaketh once, yea twice, yet man perceiveth it not"** (Job 33:14). Evidently, a *third* time is needed for humankind's slow ear.

THE SEARCH

We are going to search the Scriptures for triply, uniquely stated truths, *thrice trumpeted truths.*

Our first question was this: "Are there any?" It seems that many, if not most commentators, have ignored the numerous patterns of triples. Most truths in the Scriptures are expounded many times and in various contexts. However, we are looking for truths that are uniquely verified by three statements, three phrases or three words that are used to *thrice trumpet* a specific *truth.*

For the Scriptures to repeat a matter or truth *uniquely*, three times may seem redundant. However, such repetition affirms the truth to be a *certainty*. By stating a truth as a *triple*, God makes *certain* that ignoring this truth becomes a deliberate act of the will. Jesus Himself stated, **"Men loved darkness rather than light"** (John 3:19).

Amazingly, triples reverberate throughout the Scripture. During this study, you will be amazed, as we were, by the frequency in which God, through His writers, uniquely restates a fact or a principle three times (not four or five but three times). It is as if the Lord is saying to the hardened heart, "Did you not hear me? I said it three times!"

Contemporary literary critics teach that repetition and redundancy in writing create unnecessary clutter. However, others say that redundancy is a key to clarity.[7] Could it be that three statements are often needed for the hard-of-heeding?

Remember, it was Job's friend Elihu who displayed insight into human nature when he said: **For God speaketh once, yea twice, yet man perceiveth it not" (Job 33:14)**. (Passage quoted a third time).

Questions:

▶ How many biblical truths come to your mind that are stated three times in the same unique fashion?

▶ What about Jesus saying, **"I am[8]"** three times in John 8?

▶ Did you remember that the **"I am"** was recorded three times in the Gethsemane account?

Assignment:

Be sure to look at *Appendix A* to see the multiple repeats of God's instructions to Noah. Also, read John 1:1-14 to see if there are any triple repeats of the same identity. *Light* is included six times, so that is not a triple. It may be a double triple: two themes, each as a triple.

TRUTH: *Don't Add—Don't Diminish*

A TRUTH does not require three repetitions, but God's inspired biblical writers frequently repeat a truth to focus man's attention. The passage in 2 Peter 1:21 clearly states, **"holy men of God spake as they were moved by the Holy Ghost."**

Why are we using the phrase *thrice trumpeted truth*? Why thrice? In the Old Testament, trumpets announced praise, proclamations, or actions. Three sounds of the *Shevarim* demanded immediate attention![9]

Triples are not always in the same chapter or the same book. Here is one of our amazing foundational finds:

(1) In Deuteronomy 4:2, Moses writes God's statement:

"Ye shall not add unto the word which I command you, neither shall ye diminish ought from it, that ye may keep the

---

7   See: Brian Backman. *Thinking in Threes: The Power of Three in Writing.* Cottonwood Press. ISBN: 1-877673-67-6

8   The KJV translators inserted the word, *he* for the "I am" statements.

9   At this writing, the triple sounding can be heard: http://www.piney.com/2shevarim.au

3

commandments of the LORD your God which I command you."

(2) The second statement is also God speaking through Moses:

"What thing soever I command you, observe to do it: thou shalt not add thereto, nor diminish from it" (Deuteronomy 12:32)

(3) Interestingly, the third occurrence of this principle is not found until the very last chapter of the Book of Revelation. These are Jesus Christ's words penned by the Apostle John:

Revelation 22:18-19 "For I testify unto every man that heareth the words of the prophecy of this book, If any man shall add unto these things, God shall add unto him the plagues that are written in this book: And if any man shall take away from the words of the book of this prophecy, God shall take away his part out of the book of life, and out of the holy city, and from the things which are written in this book."

Statement one seems *clear*. The same concept restated a second time is *definite*. However, a *third*—as a final point in the closing chapter, "Don't add and don't take away" is a statement of *certainty*—including penalties.

Thrice trumpeted truths lead us to ask, "Do *triples* emanate from God's triune being?" As we will see, God's awesome being, character, and will are frequently revealed in triples. Even nature itself radiates with threes and triples. Join us in this awesome adventure as we "search the Scriptures" for scores of triples.

Section II
Foundational Triples

TRIPLES: *Certainty*

The more we studied the written Revelation, the more we recognized it to be God inspired. This section begins with a double, triply repeated biblical principle that was totally unexpected. We knew it could be found in a couple locations, but our discovery emboldened the intensity of the search to discover more *thrice trumpeted truths.*

The Old Testament Law required at least two witnesses to establish a fact, but *three* witnesses confirmed the matter as being *certain.* We knew that Moses stated this in Deuteronomy. But, surprise! He said it again, only two chapters later. Could there be a third??? Sure enough! This Old Testament principle is then referenced one more time in the Book of Hebrews. Here is what we found:

(1) **Deuteronomy** 17:6 "At the mouth of two witnesses, or three witnesses, shall he that is worthy of death be put to death; but at the mouth of one witness he shall not be put to death."

(2) **Deuteronomy** 19:15 "One witness shall not rise up against a man for any iniquity, or for any sin, in any sin that he sinneth: at the mouth of two witnesses, or at the mouth of three witnesses, shall the matter be established."

The following passage from the book of Hebrews is a direct reference to the Old Testament Law and is included in this first triple.

(3) **Hebrews** 10:28 "He that despised Moses' law died without mercy under two or three witnesses:"

The next question: does the New Testament itself, repeat this same principle three times? Indeed! This discovery was the clue that we had "found" a pattern that needed serious investigation! The references, one by Jesus and two by Paul:

(1) **Matthew** 18:16 "But if he will not hear thee, then take with thee one or two more, that in the mouth of two or three witnesses every word may be established."

(2) **2 Corinthians** 13:1 "This is the third time I am coming to you. In the mouth of two or three witnesses shall every word be established."

(3) 1 Timothy 5:19 "Against an elder receive not an accusation, but before two or <u>three</u> witnesses."

A Pattern: These two triples of a *biblical principle* were among the first that we discovered. As a result, our method of study became more focused and we realized that we needed to develop a method for the study. It developed as *three key questions:*

▶ Do three witnesses show us that God is *confirming a truth*, that it is *certain* and unavoidable?

▶ Do the Scriptures provide numerous *thrice trumpeted truths* providing evidence for the *divine inspiration* of the Scriptures?

▶ Do *thrice trumpeted truths* notify individual readers/hearers/learners that he/she is *without excuse???*

Our appetites of curiosity were rewarded with an awesome display of numerous *thrice trumpeted truths* evidencing *TRUTH's certainty*.

TRIPLES: *In Genesis 1:1*

What did we find? It was captivating to note that God began His written revelation with a triple: **"In the beginning *[time]* God created the heaven *[space]* and the earth *[matter]*"** (see *Creation*).

God created this time, space and matter universe for human habitation and also to manifest His **"eternal power and godhead."**[10]

So, did the first triple satisfy us? No, and the triples seemed to leap at us. It was amazing! The first triple produced more!

• *Time:* past, present, future (Three perceptions).

• *Space:* length, width, height (Three dimensions).

• *Matter:* proton, neutron, electron (Three basic particles).

Note: Other sub-particles are evidenced but are not basic.

Should we be surprised if the Triune Creator were to fill His creation with triples? Some of our findings were almost an *eureka* moment. We discovered that contemporary science and its study of the natural world has identified multiple patterns of triples.

• The natural *states of matter:* solid, liquid, gas.

• The primary *colors:* red, blue, yellow. Combinations can produce all other colors.

---

[10] "For the invisible things of him from the creation of the world are clearly seen, being understood by the things that are made, even his eternal power and Godhead; so that they are without excuse" (Romans 1:20).

- The *seed* consists of three main parts: seed coat, embryo, food tissue.

Loyola University professor, John A. McNulty, Ph.D[11], has developed a listing of at least 130 sets of triples in human anatomy. For example:

- Three layers of skin: dermis, epidermis, subcutaneous.
- Three bones (ossicles) of the ear: malleus (hammer), incus (anvil), stapes (stirrup).
- Three types of joints: fibrous, cartilaginous, synovial.

Dr. McNulty included five sets of threes in embryology and 32 sets of threes in the human head. Additional occurrences of triples in nature include the following:

- The triad elements: carbon, nitrogen, oxygen (there are others).
- The mathematical tessellations: translation, rotation, reflection.
- The garden flower: annuals, biennials, perennials.

There are scores more: how about a three leaf clover or the discovery that water flows over a sill as three distinct currents? How about the discovery that there seem to be three natural forms of DNA (a, B and Z)?

We discovered more detail related to creation. Many of these are included in the sections: *God's Work in Creation* and *God's Image in Man*.

Questions:

▶ Why would some say that the multitude of triples in the human body is accidental?

▶ Can you think of an entire passage or specific truth that is uniquely repeated three times in the Scriptures?

▶ Doesn't the use of *"Word"* three times in John 1:1 confirm Jesus Christ as being the revealed *Word* of God?

TRIPLES: *In Doctrine*

So what was next? What about the most basic of doctrines? Might there be triples that trumpet God's revelation, manifestations of Himself, and/ or of His attributes?

---

[11] http://www.meddean.luc.edu/lumen/MedEd/GrossAnatomy/Threes. html

TRIPLE *WORD*

We knew that *word* was used in three ways and that God has communicated to mankind by three specific revelations, each described as **The Word**. (This was a triple).

(1) God *spoke*: "And God <u>said</u> . . . ."[12] This was "The **Word** of His power." This was *creation*.

(2) God has also given us His *written* **Word**.[13]

(3) God's greatest revelation of Himself is through *His Son*—The **Word**.[14]

(1) The *Word* of His Power. The first revelation that God gave was through His work of *creation*. This has been called *natural revelation*,[15] that is, God has revealed His eternal power and godhead[16] through the awesome creation evidenced in nature.

The *word* of creation: Richard Swenson's four part video series, *More than Meets the Eye*, begins each section with the phrase: "**God spoke to the void, and the universe showed up!**"[17]

Here are three passages that relate God's speaking (word) to the creation and then to His sustaining power over His creation:

▶ Genesis 1:3 "And God <u>said</u>, let there be light."

▶ Hebrews 1:3 "and upholding all things by the <u>word of his power</u>."[18]

▶ 2 Peter 3:5-7 "For this they willingly are ignorant of, that by the <u>word</u> of God the heavens were of old, and the earth standing out of the water and in the water: Whereby the world that then was, being overflowed with water, perished: But the heavens

---

12   Genesis 1:3, 6, 9, 11, 14, 20, 24, 26

13   Hebrews 4:12

14   John 1:14

15   Some use the term *general revelation* to include God evidencing of Himself in creation, in history, and through conscience.

16   Romans 1:20 "For the invisible things of him from the creation of the world are clearly seen, being understood by the things that are made, even his <u>eternal power and Godhead</u>; so that they are without excuse."

17   Richard Swenson, http://www.richardswenson.org/dvd-videos/science-a-sovereignty-of-god.html

18   Colossians 1:17 "And he is before all things, and by him all things consist."

and the earth, which are now, by the same <u>word</u> are **kept in store, reserved unto fire against the day of judgment and perdition of ungodly men.**"[19]

God spoke the universe into existence and He continues to uphold it "**by the <u>word</u> of his power.**"

Note: Can we imagine Adam's and Eve's communion with God as they marveled at/in the "good" creation? They even "*heard* the voice of God walking in the garden."[20] God was "voicing" with them.

Could God's "voicing" have included theological instruction and an account of creation? Also, through the creation they could see His awesome ability to make and sustain everything. They did not have the "scientific" insight of modern human knowledge—but their knowledge did point them to God. *Human* "wisdom" today attempts to move away from God.[21]

However, for anyone who is really looking, God's creative wisdom, power, and glory are evidenced throughout all of nature. The psalmist goes beyond simple evidence—he says it is a *declaration*!

Psalm 19:1, 2 "**The heavens <u>declare</u> the glory of God; and the firmament sheweth his handywork. Day unto day uttereth speech.**"

(2) The Written *Word* is the second revelation of God. It reveals His character, His purposes, and His plans.[22] (Note: the revelation of God in nature through His creation is *insufficient* to find God's plan of salvation). The psalmist again speaks to the significance (a four) of the written revelation: "**The <u>law</u> of the LORD is perfect, converting the soul: the <u>testimony</u> of the LORD is sure, making wise the simple. The <u>statutes</u> of the LORD are right, rejoicing the heart: the <u>commandment</u> of the LORD is pure, enlightening the eyes**" (Psalm 19:7-8).

---

[19] Note the triple: "world that then was," "earth which is now," and "new heavens and a new earth" (verse 13).

[20] Genesis 3:8

[21] 1 Corinthians 2:14 "But the natural man receiveth not the things of the Spirit of God: for they are foolishness unto him: neither can he know them, because they are spiritually discerned."

[22] 2 Timothy 3:15-16 "All scripture is given by inspiration of God, and is profitable for doctrine, for reproof, for correction, for instruction in righteousness:"

Scores of passages proclaim this revelation as being inspired by God. Here are three:

▶ John 17:17 "Thy word is truth."

▶ 2 Timothy 3:15-16 "All scripture is given by inspiration of God, and is profitable for doctrine, for reproof, for correction, for instruction in righteousness:"

▶ 2 Peter 1:21 "For the prophecy came not in old time by the will of man: but holy men of God spake as they were moved by the Holy Ghost."

When we read and study the revealed *truth* that God has both given and preserved for us, we bow in awe at God's love and concern for the human race. He has made diligent effort to clearly communicate to us by giving us a written, preserved Book.

Questions:

▶ Why is a written revelation of truth[23] needed?

Consider this: humanity has only two sources for gaining information:

■ *observation*[24] of our perceivable universe and human knowledge.

■ *reasoning* ability.

We know that *neither* source can answer questions of eternal values: Is there a God? Why am I here? Where am I going? Which conduct is right? Which is wrong or has dire consequences?[25]

▶ Why do you think so many people refuse to accept the truths that God has revealed?

▶ Some neither want to "look" at the Ten Commandments nor want others to be able to see them. Why not?

---

[23] http://www.3-truths.com

[24] This broad definition of "observation" includes discovered information that is handed down from learned to learner. This is limited: 1 Corinthians 2:7-9.

[25] "But as it is written, Eye hath not seen, nor ear heard, neither have entered into the heart of man, the things which God hath prepared for them that love him." (1 Corinthians 2:9)

(3) The Incarnate *Word* [26] is the third and most revealing of God's love for the entire human race. This revelation was Jesus Christ, the promised *Messiah*. He came to manifest God's love for humankind and to deliver from the power, penalty and ultimately, the presence of sin. Also, we noted a triple use of *"Word"* in the first verse of John's Gospel: "In the beginning was the **Word**, and the **Word** was with God, and the **Word** was God" (John 1:1).

John continues and identifies the *"Word"* as referring to Jesus: "And the **Word** was made flesh, and dwelt among us, (and we beheld his glory, the glory as of the only begotten of the Father,) full of grace and truth" (John 1:14).

The *Word* is Jesus Christ. Interestingly, John in his first epistle also identifies the **Word** as *the Word of Life*: "That which was from the beginning *[the beginning of Jesus' ministry]*, which we have heard, which we have seen with our eyes, which we have looked upon, and our hands have handled, of the **Word of life**" (1 John 1:1).

Note the triple: *heard, seen, touched.* John is clearly *trumpeting* the truth that Jesus Christ did come to earth and John *heard* Him teach, *saw* Him perform miracles, and was so near that he actually *touched* the Lord Jesus. The reality of Jesus Christ coming to earth as a man is triply confirmed by this passage.

TRIPLE: *Attributes*

God revealed Himself as Father, Son and Holy Spirit: each possess the same divine attributes and each is worthy of adoration, of worship, and of our faith. [27]

Imagine our fascination when we realized there are three specific attributes that describe God's *being*. [28] We list one passage to illustrate

---

[26]   *Creation*: Natural Revelation.
       Word: Biblical Revelation.
       Jesus Christ: Personal Revelation.
[27]   Hebrews 11:6 "But without faith it is impossible to please him: for he that cometh to God must believe that he is, and that he is a rewarder of them that diligently seek him."
[28]   These thee describe His *being*. However, God's attributes are many. He is eternal, infinite, self-existent, spirit, truth, changeless, holy, love, light, life, merciful, gracious and others.

each of these three. However, throughout Scripture this triple truth is evidenced in many passages and multiple settings.

(1) Omniscient: God is all-knowing.

"He telleth the number of the stars; he calleth them all by their names. Great is our Lord, and of great power: his understanding is <u>infinite</u>." (Psalm 147:4, 5)

(2) Omnipotent: God is all-powerful.

"But Jesus beheld them, and said unto them, With men this is impossible; but with God all things are <u>possible</u>." (Matthew 19:26)

(3) Omnipresent: God is all-present, everywhere.

"Whither shall I go from thy spirit? or whither shall I flee from thy presence?

If I ascend up into heaven, thou art there: if I make my bed in hell *[sheol]*, behold, thou art <u>there</u>.

If I take the wings of the morning, and dwell in the uttermost parts of the sea; <u>Even there</u> shall thy hand lead me, and thy right hand shall hold me.

If I say, Surely the darkness shall cover me; even the night shall be light about me. Yea, the darkness hideth not from thee; but the night shineth as the day: the darkness and the light are both alike to thee." (Psalm 139:7-12)

(See also Matthew 18:20 and Matthew 28:20).

Observation:

These three attributes trumpet God's creative/sustaining ability. His *omnipresence* accounts for the vastness of the universe. His *omnipotence* accounts for the energy input: the energy/mass/light creation. His *omniscience* enabled the design of life and replication by DNA molecules. DNA—a unique code for each plant type and for each animal kind.[29]

God is creator and sustainer of the universe and also of His human creation. I can truthfully say: "He is my God, my Savior, my Lord. His attributes strengthen my faith. His attributes trumpet the fact that He is

---

[29] Werner Gitt identifies the vast amount of information that was required as input for the totality of the universe and all life forms.
In the Beginning was Information, Master Books, 2005, ISBN 0890514615

able to completely fulfill His will for every believer—and for me! I can sleep well at night and I can trust Him for each new day."

Praise: The *Doxology* is a song of praise and adoration to our great God. Let us sing it in His presence as we worship Him.

Questions:

▶ God's three revelations as the *Word* each proclaim His existence and being. Could this be an indication of His love for us and of His desire that we know who He is?

▶ God is omniscient, omnipotent, and omnipresent. Shouldn't that knowledge help us to realize His creative, sustaining, and redeeming ability?

▶ If God knows everything about my life and my needs—why should I pray?

God wants us to recognize our dependence on Him. He wants us to worship Him because of His greatness and of His love for us.

TRIPLE: *Holy*

The fact of God's holiness is a cardinal doctrine. Are there any triples that trumpet this truth? We knew that the phrase, "Holy, holy, holy" would be displayed as an awesome triple. But, how many times is the phrase found? Could it be three?

(1) The first "Holy, holy, holy" was recorded by Isaiah in chapter six. Isaiah described his experience:

"In the year that king Uzziah died I saw also the Lord sitting upon a throne, high and lifted up, and his train filled the temple. Above it stood the seraphims: each one had six wings; with twain he covered his face, and with twain he covered his feet, and with twain he did fly. *[Note three sets of wings]* And one cried unto another, and said,

Holy, holy, holy, is the LORD of hosts: the whole earth is full of his glory" (Isaiah 6:1-3).

The Seraphim (angels) could only worship God's awesome holiness. Their words were: "Holy, holy, holy." Each "Holy" is a statement of Divine Grandeur—one "Holy" for each member of the Trinity.

Isaiah then bowed in guilt before God's holiness. He recorded his response: "Then said I, Woe is me! for I am undone; because I am a man of unclean lips, and I dwell in the midst of a people of unclean lips: for mine eyes have seen the King, the LORD of hosts" (Isaiah 6:5).

Isaiah made three confessions:

(1) I am a man (alienation from God);

(2) I have unclean lips (impurity when compared to God);

(3) I dwell with people of unclean lips (pollution because of the sinful culture).

When Isaiah saw the awesomeness of God's holiness, he realized both his own sinfulness and the sinfulness of his people. It is obvious that people who reject God or who use His name vainly do not realize who He really is.

(2) The praise phrase, **"Holy, holy, holy"** is sounded a second time as a triumphant proclamation in Revelation chapter four. The Apostle John writes the description of his heavenly vision:

> "And the four beasts *[living creatures, probably seraphim]* had each of them six wings about him; and they were full of eyes within: and they rest not day and night, saying,
>
> **Holy, holy, holy,** Lord God Almighty, which <u>was</u>, and <u>is</u>, and <u>is to come</u>." (Revelation 4:8)

The angelic response continues as two triples.

> "And when those beasts *[angels]* give <u>glory</u> and <u>honour</u> and <u>thanks</u> to him that sat on the throne, who liveth for ever and ever, . . . and cast their crowns before the throne, saying,
>
> Thou art worthy, O Lord, to receive <u>glory</u> and <u>honour</u> and <u>power</u>: for thou hast created all things, and for thy pleasure they are and were created." (Revelation 4:9—11)[30]

(3) The third: Since this study relates to triples, it would be expected that we would find a third "Holy, Holy, Holy." But, we couldn't find a third!

Please allow a speculative question: Could it be that the *third* awesomely, worshipful praise, "Holy, holy, holy," will be by another heavenly host like the one described in Revelation 5:13? Will there be a third proclamation: Holy, holy, holy that will include all the redeemed?[31]

Note: God commands mankind *five* times: **"Be ye holy, for I am holy."**[32] Such an order seems impossible for anyone to attain.

---

[30]   Note: for the curious, look for some triples in Revelation chapter 1. Are there nine? How about chapters 4 & 5?

[31]   There are some other twos in the Scripture that possibly await a third, with all the redeemed involved. See: http://www.3-truths.com

[32]   Found *five* times: Leviticus 11:44; 11:45; 19:2; 20:26; 1 Peter 1:16.

God is holy and humankind is NOT holy. The human lack of holiness is labeled as sin. **"For all have sinned, and come short of the glory of God"** (Romans 3:23).

But, there is *good news!* God is not only holy, He is also a God of love for humankind. Thus, God made a provision whereby individuals, by faith, can be made holy through God's plan. Jesus Christ came to earth, so that, by faith[33] in Christ's atonement, any individual may have sins forgiven and be made righteous in God's eyes (see *The Gospel*).

Question:

Has our initial search for triples stimulated your interest in finding more of these unique triples that proclaim *certain* truth in God's *triple* revelation: the *Word* of His power, the written *Word*, the *Word*, Jesus Christ.

---

[33]   Another *trumpeted truth:* "The just shall live by faith" (Habakkuk 2:4; Romans 1:16; Galatians 3:11; Hebrews 10:38).

Some Questions

▶ When you read an objective, "To find triples in Scripture," what kinds of triples come to your mind?

▶ For a group study adventure: how many triples can you think of that are found in nature?

▶ How many additional triples can you find in the first three chapters of Genesis?

▶ Before looking at the section concerning Jesus' trial before Pilate, how many triples can you find in John's account (John 18, 19)?

▶ How many trials were there?

Part Two
God

Section I
God is One

After our initial discoveries, we determined to look for triples related to God Himself. So we ask: Are there any triples used to reveal God's being?

God began His revelation to mankind by a simple statement: "In the beginning God . . ." (Genesis 1:1). God's existence is the foundational declaration. Then our findings became spectacular as triples concerning God's being and attributes began to be uncovered. We found multiple triples *trumpeting*: there is ONE God, that He is triune, and that His works image this triune attribute.

While the Scriptures abound with evidence that God is triune, even more emphatic are the repeated affirmations clearly showing there is only *one God*.

ONE GOD

The Scriptures clearly declare that there is one and only one God. We found this to be a *thrice trumped truth* because we located three descriptive phrases: *One Lord, One God,* and *One,* each, itself resulting in a triple.

(1) ONE LORD: The phrase, "One Lord," is found three times:

- **One Lord:** "Hear, O Israel: The LORD our God is one LORD" (Deuteronomy 6:4).

- **One Lord:** "And the LORD shall be king over all the earth: in that day shall there be one LORD, and his name one" (Zechariah 14:9).

- **One Lord:** "And Jesus answered him, The first of all the commandments is, Hear, O Israel; The Lord our God is one Lord" (Mark 12:29).[34]

---

[34] "There is One God and He is One." The mathematician frequently uses the phrase, "one and only one," to indicate that the attribute of *oneness* is unique.

(2) ONE GOD: This attribute of God's being one is stated three times in the New Testament:

- **One God:** ". . . one God and Father of all, who is above all, and through all, and in you all" (Ephesians 4:6).
- **One God:** "But to us there is but one God, the Father, of whom are all things, and we in him; and one Lord Jesus Christ, by whom are all things, and we by him" (1 Corinthians 8:6).
- **One God:** "For there is one God, and one mediator between God and men, the man Christ Jesus" (1 Timothy 2:5).

NOTE: Since there is only one God and there is no other God, we are not torn between two or three or more gods. We can give our undivided love, devotion, and worship to our one God. "Thou shalt have no other gods before Me" (Exodus 20:3).

(3) ONE: God's being is *One*. We found three biblical references to God being only ONE:

- **"God is one"** "Now a mediator is not a mediator of one, but God is one" (Galatians 3:20).
- **"One Mediator"** The New Testament states there is One Mediator: "For there is one God, and one mediator between God and men, the man Christ Jesus" (1 Timothy 2:5).
- **"No other Gods"** "Thou shalt have no other gods before me" (Exodus 20:3).

Question: What else could God have done or said to make it clear that there is the one and only God?

> *Answer:* Then we found Isaiah 45:5-22, a most interesting passage.
> God seems to repeat the *oneness* truth, using multiple sets of triples.
> I found this passage by a computer search. It looked interesting so
> I turned to the passage and began to read. Then *three* triples almost
> leaped from the page. Here was a *certainty*, thrice, triply stated.

"I am the LORD, There is None Else!"

Our study group looked at the passage in Isaiah 45, and we were all fascinated when we began to examine the repeats—several doubles, many triples, and a couple of fours. Here are three sets of triples from this passage which clearly emphasize God's uniqueness.

- I am the LORD, *v5*.
- I am the LORD, *v6*.

- I am the LORD, *v18*.
    - there is none else, *v5*.
    - there is none else, *v6*.
    - there is none else, *v22*.
        - Thus saith the LORD, *v11*.
        - Thus saith the LORD, *v13*.
        - Thus saith the LORD, *v14*.

Question: Can you find more triples in Isaiah 45:5-22? There are more! Hebrew poetry frequently uses doubles. This passage is amazing. We could not help but acclaim divine authorship to these ancient poetic writings. It became evident that the LORD was attempting to clarify the truth of His oneness and majesty.

Note: Israel, as the representative of all humanity, consistently failed to acknowledge their *ONE* God. They made and worshiped idols of all kinds with all kinds of "worship" rituals. Even now, humankind is consistent in its service to self, sin and Satan. Each of these pushes God away.

The commentary on Commandment Two states: "**I the Lord thy God am a jealous God.**" He is saying that He is to be worshiped and honored and nothing else is to take first place. The passage goes on to say that when people give first allegiance to any other, even the children will suffer consequences.

Concerning the worship of other gods, God clearly stated: "**Thou shalt not bow down thyself to them, nor serve them: for I the LORD thy God am a jealous God, visiting the iniquity of the fathers upon the children unto the third and fourth generation of them that hate me; And shewing mercy unto thousands of them that love me, and keep my commandments**" (Exodus 20:5-6).

This truth, that the wickedness of parents has its consequences in the lives of the children, has been evidenced throughout history. It is the children who suffer when their adults do not follow God's directives to a godly, joyful life.

Questions:

▶ In what ways might children suffer the consequences of parents' sins? Note a paradox: While children are influenced by parents, peers, and professors, each individual will give account of himself to God (see Ezekiel 18:1-4).

▶ What are some of the "gods" that people in our modern culture place before God?

▶ In what ways should the phrase concerning *showing mercy* be a comfort to any individual who decides to break an evil consequence chain by receiving personal forgiveness and following God's directives?

Next: As we continued to look at truths surrounding God Himself we looked at the foundational *triple*. God is *Trinity* and then we found that He has on *three* occasions manifested Himself as Trinity.

Section II

God is Trinity

Now to the incomprehensible: the truth that God is *One*, yet He has revealed Himself as being *Trinity*. We all knew that this truth is clearly taught in the New Testament and alluded to in the Old Testament. However, little did we realize that the Scriptures reveal this key doctrine as a *thrice trumpeted, triply depicted truth* of God being *Trinity*. This was a surprise that none of our group had identified with a triple.

The descriptive word, *trinity*, has been assigned to this revelation of God's existence. The word, *trinity* is formed, because tri = three; unity = one; *God is one*! Yet, He is Father, Son, and Holy Spirit.

Concrete analogies do not assist our understanding of God or of His triune being. Someone said that water is manifest in three states: ice, water, steam. That is not an adequate illustration. A misunderstanding occurs when we try to look at the three as 1 + 1 + 1. However some have said we should consider the fact that 1 x 1 x 1 = 1. This is also inadequate, but it does move the focus away from a simple addition concept.[35]

There is nothing in nature to describe God's triune existence other than a tri-partite view of *God's image* in man: body, soul, spirit.[36] Then how can we describe the Trinity? A simple statement is the most accurate and this author has used the following statement numerous times: "God is One and has revealed Himself as being Father, Son, and Holy Spirit." End of description! Anything added can generate confusion, especially for children.

Human experience and/or logical reasoning cannot comprehend this.[37] However, we found three manifestations of God's self-identification as Trinity.

---

[35] Yes, multiplication can be viewed as a function of addition.

[36] Note: Countless books on theology have been written throughout the centuries that proclaim and defend this central Bible doctrine. Yet, the doctrine of the Trinity is often the first doctrine to "go" when cultists devise a new religious system.

[37] The human experience and intellect is limited in its foundation to comprehend the Three in One. Therefore, no one should try to use

As we investigated manifestations of God, we began in the Old Testament. There were several appearances of angelic beings but our findings centered on God manifesting Himself in human form.

Questions:

▶ Can you recall any Old Testament events in which God appeared in the form of a man (a theophany).

Note: In the New Testament it becomes evident that these appearances were really a christophany, an appearance of the pre-incarnate Christ.

▶ How many such appearances were there in the Old Testament?

GOD: *Manifest*

The awe continued as we found that there were *three* and only three times in which God, as the Pre-incarnate Christ, appeared in a *human form* to *His people.* If the Old Testament books were written by non-inspired authors, it would seem logical to find numerous occasions to help support their religious ideas. But there are three and only three to people of God. The three manifestations:

- To Abraham, as *One* of the three men in Genesis 18:1-33.[38]
- To Jacob, when he wrestled with the *Man* in Genesis 32:24-29.
- To Joshua, as *Captain* of the host of LORD in Joshua 5:13-15.

Abraham, Jacob and Joshua were chosen of God for a specific task: Abraham, as father of the Hebrew peoples; Jacob, as father of the Israelite nation; Joshua, as their leader into the Promised Land.[39] Evidently, God wanted His chosen people to be fully aware of His reality.

The Fourth Man: There is another interesting encounter which some believe to be an angel like the angel who later delivered Daniel. However, some think this appearance to be that of the pre-incarnate Christ. The translators did use the phrase: "Son of God."[40]

---

inadequate, misleading illustrations. If there were any kind of illustration available, God would, no doubt, have used it.

[38] God also spoke to Abraham and/or other "dreams," but this is the only human form.

[39] God had appeared to Moses, but not as a physical, human form.

[40] Daniel 3:25 (KJV & NKJV)

This fourth event was to the "Gentile" Nebuchadnezzar, as the fourth *man* in the fire in Daniel 3:25. Nebuchadnezzar was the "King of the world." He had conquered and destroyed Jerusalem and had taken most surviving residents into the Babylonian captivity. The Jews were in his control, but remained under God's ultimate protection.

As a result of Nebuchadnezzar's encounter with the forth "Man," Nebuchadnezzar issued the decree: **"Therefore I make a decree, That every people, nation, and language, which speak any thing amiss against the God of Shadrach, Meshach, and Abed-nego, shall be cut in pieces, and their houses shall be made a dunghill: because there is no other God that can deliver after this sort"** (Daniel 3:29).

The providential outcome of that encounter: the Jews were miraculously preserved during the seventy year captivity. Then, after seventy years they were permitted to return to their Promised Land. Not all chose to return.[41]

Note: There were other occasions in which the pre-incarnate Christ evidenced Himself,[42] or spoke, or revealed His glory in non-human form. (The cloud by day and the fire by night were manifestations of God's reality, but not as a *human form*).

Question: Before reading further, can you recall occasions during Jesus' time on earth in which Father, Son, and Holy Spirit were manifested together?

THE TRINITY: *Manifest*

We were thrilled by another spectacular realization. Again a three! We found three occasions in which Father, Son and Holy Spirit manifest themselves during Jesus' time on earth: Jesus' baptism, the transfiguration, and in the Temple during Jesus' final week.

This triple becomes a revelation of *certainty* for God being Trinity.

(1) At Jesus' **Baptism:** This is the first clear trumpeting of the truth: Father, Son, Holy Spirit are God.

"And <u>Jesus</u>, when he was baptized, went up straightway out of the water: and, lo, the heavens were opened unto him, and he

---

[41]   *Ezra* and *Nehemiah* record events surrounding the returns.

[42]   Some might claim other encounters, especially to Moses on the mountain (Exodus 33:20-23). However, they do not seem to be as a "bodied" person.

saw the <u>Spirit of God</u> descending like a dove, and lighting upon him: And lo <u>a voice</u> from heaven, saying, This is my beloved Son, in whom I am well pleased" (Matthew 3:16, 17).

- The **Father** spoke.
- The **Son** was visible.
- The **Holy Spirit** appeared as a Dove.

Note: This event is recorded in three Gospels.
(Matthew 3:16, 17; Mark 1:11; Luke 3:22)

(2) At Jesus' **Transfiguration:** Matthew provides the second proclamation: Father, Son, Holy Spirit.

"While he yet spake, behold, a bright <u>cloud</u> overshadowed them: and behold a <u>voice</u> out of the cloud, which said, This is my beloved <u>Son</u>, in whom I am well pleased; hear ye him." (Matthew 17:5)

- The **Father** was heard.
- The **Son** was visible.
- The **Holy Spirit** as a "bright cloud overshadowed them."

(See also Mark 9:7).

(3) In the **Temple:** This event begins with Jesus' simple prayer:

"Father, glorify thy name.

Then came there a voice from heaven, saying, I have both glorified it, and will glorify it again . . . .

And I, if I be lifted up from the earth, will <u>draw</u> all men unto me." (John 12:28-32)

Note: the drawing ministry is the work of the Holy Spirit.

- The **Father** spoke—The people said, "It thundered."
- The **Son** was visible.
- The **Holy Spirit**—Jesus speaks of the ministry of the Holy Spirit[43] when He stated: "Will <u>draw</u> all men unto Me."

It is spectacularly amazing that there were *three* recorded events in which the Father, Son, and Holy Spirit were portrayed.[44] This record cannot be an accident. God provided the readers of His Scriptures with the triple

---

[43] The Holy Spirit's ministry also includes *convicting.* John 16:7-11

[44] These three manifestations of Father, Son, and Holy Spirit used three non-related symbols to indicate that there is nothing within human comprehension that can be used to adequately illustrate the Three as One.

account so that we can be *certain* of God's Triune Being. We must stand in awe of these manifestations.

Questions:

▶ Are there any Old Testament references that indicate Trinity? (See Isaiah 42:1) Might there be two others?

▶ Why do you think that most cults reject God as being Trinity?[45]

▶ Can you think of some additional triples in God's creation (in nature)?

Note: If God were not Trinity—He could not have demonstrated His love and concern for humankind through Jesus Christ. Without Jesus Christ, the meaning of John 3:16 would have no significance. Salvation through Christ's death, burial, and resurrection would not have been possible.

---

[45] Some commentators have identified an "unholy-trinity" in the Book of Revelation: *Satan*, the *anti-christ [the beast]*, and the *false prophet*. Satan, via the anti-christ and the false prophet attempts a "last stand" against God. But, God wins (Revelation 19:19-20:3).

Some Questions

These questions relate to *The Feasts of the Lord.* These feasts were another amazing discovery in our search for triples. However, they are not included in this publication. The study was fascinating!

- ▶ How many Spring Feasts of the Lord were to be observed?
- ▶ How many Fall Feast of the Lord were to be observed?
- ▶ How many of the seven Feasts of the Lord were to people to observe at the Tabernacle/Temple?
- ▶ Why do you think all of the Spring Feasts were always observed within a six day period?
- ▶ Which day of the week began the Feast of Firstfruits?
- ▶ Which day of the week was to be the Feast of Pentecost? It was 50 days after which day? (By our method of counting days, it would be the 49th day).
- ▶ How many days did Jesus stay in Jerusalem after His parents left for home (Luke 2)?
- ▶ How many Passover feasts did Jesus attend during His ministry?

For more commentary:
http://www.3-truths.com

Section III
Creation's Triples

We saw that God's being, not only is Tri-unity but we also found that His creation and creatures emanate of threes! As we moved our inquiry to the creation account and to nature itself, our speculation that triads radiate from God's very being was strengthened. Even in music, the *triad* is the basic harmonic cord. How about the three primary colors matched with the three color receptors in the cone cells of the eye: red, blue, and yellow? It would take several zillion years for that match up to "evolve."

So, let's begin with nature itself. The natural world is not here by accident neither are the triples in the creation account accidental. Here are three passages that clearly *trumpet* the creation fact:

Genesis 1:1 "In the beginning God <u>created</u> . . . ."

Psalm 148:4-5 "Praise him, ye heavens of heavens, and ye waters that be above the heavens. Let them praise the name of the LORD: for he commanded, and they were <u>created</u>."

Colossians 1:16, 17 "For by him were all things created, that are in heaven, and that are in earth, visible and invisible, whether they be thrones, or dominions, or principalities, or powers: all things were <u>created</u> by him, and for him: And he is before all things, and by him all things consist."

If we were to list all of the passages that speak of God creating, many pages could be filled. The Scriptures clearly declare God as Creator.

Questions:

► If there were a witness to the origin of the natural universe, would people believe the witness? How about three witnesses: Father, Son and Holy Spirit?

► Why do you think many believe that "something" exploded with the result being the universe?

For something to go "bang," it had to exist. Therefore, the "big bang" people evidently believe that something was there. Yet, they refuse to accept God's revelation that He is the eternal One, or that *He* was there in the beginning.

► What are some implications of believing that unplanned "blind chance" caused both the universe and the DNA of life to form?

Observations:

▶ God stated that He created all. This claim extends to the totality of reality: seen and unseen, perceivable and un-perceivable.

▶ God gave us senses with the ability to perceive within our time, space, matter arena and to live within the reality that God created.

Dr. Richard Swenson's four part video series, *More Than Meets the Eye,*[46] begins each section with the spectacular proclamation: "***God spoke to the void, and the universe showed up!***"

THE COSMOS

Are there any other triples evidenced in the universe? We have already listed a few in nature, but now we want to look at details and a few implications. We review the opening statement: "In the <u>beginning</u> *[time]* God created the <u>heaven</u> *[space]* and the <u>earth</u> *[matter]*."

The account of the universe and humankind's place in it begins with a definitive word, created.[47] This is the *first* of three uses of the Hebrew word *[bara]* create. God created *[bara]* our perceivable habitat consisting of three entities: time, space, matter.

(1) Time: "the *beginning*"

Interestingly, time consists of three reality perceptions: *past, present, future.*

God created time for us, not for Himself because He is eternal and His *existence* is in the eternal *"NOW."*

● What we experienced as *past* is God's *now.*

● What we experience as *now* is God's *now.*

● What we will experience in the *future* or for those who will follow us is God's *now.*

God's existence is in the eternal *"NOW."*

Paul speaks of past, present and future: ". . . all these things happened *[past]* unto them for ensamples: and they are written *[present]* for our admonition, upon whom the ends of the world are come. Wherefore let him that thinketh he standeth *[present]* take heed lest he fall *[future]*" (1 Corinthians 10:11-12).

---

[46] Richard Swenson. http://www.richardswenson.com

[47] *Ex-nihilo.* From nothing. It is interesting to note that people with a naturalistic mind set are almost forced to believe in the eternality of matter-energy. Yet they seem unable to recognize the eternality of God or of His eternal creating/sustaining power.

Paul summarizes God's regenerating work of the redeemed by citing past, present, and future: "Among whom also we all had our conversation in times <u>past</u> in the lusts of our flesh, fulfilling the desires of the flesh . . . But God, who is rich in mercy, for his great love wherewith he loved us, Even when we were dead in sins, hath quickened us together with Christ, (by grace ye are saved;) And hath raised us up together, and made us sit together in heavenly places in Christ Jesus: *[past and continuing present]* That in the ages to come *[future]* he might shew the exceeding riches of his grace in his kindness toward us through Christ Jesus. For by grace are ye saved through faith; and that not of yourselves: it is the gift of God: Not of works, lest any man should boast" (Ephesians 2:3-9).

God created time for humankind's actions, perceptions, and accountability. Could it be that people who do not want to consider the truth that God created, are fearful of their *future* accountability? That accountability could require a report as to how we used our time. The little poem says it all.

> I have only just a minute,
> only 60 seconds in it.
> Forced upon me, can't refuse it.
> Didn't seek it, didn't choose it
> But it's up to me to use it.
> I must suffer if I lose it.
> Give account if I abuse it.
> Just a tiny little minute,
> But eternity is in it. [48]

Humankind was created and placed in time. Time's reality is unique for us. We cannot move in it. We cannot visit the past. We cannot perceive the future. We are in the constant *now*. For us, the past is gone; the future is unperceivable. We do not know when our earthbound *now* will end. James spoke to this: "Whereas ye know not what shall be on the morrow. For what is your life? It is even a vapour, that appeareth for a little time, and then vanisheth away. For that ye ought to say, If the Lord will, we shall live, and do this, or that" (James 4:14-15).

---

[48] "*I have only just a minute,*" by English teacher Welcome McCullough, Saugus, Massachusetts in the 40's. Quoted by Benjamin Mays (1894-1984). Quoted by J. Mark Holland, *Public Speaking Course*, Spring, 1955. Popularized by Willie Jolley (1956 -).

God is eternal. He has *always been and always will be.* Such a statement is time-related for our comprehension, but God acts in His eternal existence and is not limited by our time frame. He created time for the time, space, matter universe. Time does not use up a part of eternity; it is not a segment of *eternity.* God's design of time did not place limitations on His eternality any more than His creation of the earth limits Him to our planet.

Yet, for us the *now* is here and Paul stated that *now* is the time for salvation: "behold, **now** is the accepted time; behold, **now** is the day of salvation" (2 Corinthians 6:2).

Paul also speaks of "**Redeeming the time**" (Ephesians 5:16). The Psalmist confessed, "**My times are in Thy hands**" (Psalm 31:15).

Conclusion: We cannot move either forward or backward in time. Interestingly, our *past* can influence both the present and the future; our *present* can influence the future. Also, we can learn from both our past and the past of others. We learn from history so that we can avoid errors and follow successful examples. Therefore, let us use our *now* for the glory of our creator and according to His directives.

(2) Space: "the heaven(s)"

The heaven is the second listed entity in the creation account.

There are *three* dimensions of space: *length, breadth, height.*

In the descriptive language of mathematics, the numeral "3" is used to denote the three equal dimensions of a cube (x^3).

It is interesting to note that the Holy of Holies in the Tabernacle was to be constructed in the shape of a cube.

While God does not permit us to move within the three components of time, He does allow human beings and most animal life to move within the three dimensional *space* that we perceive: forward, backward; up, down; or sideways.

During preparation studies, I found an intriguing non-three. Paul uses a fourth[49] dimensional illustration for the believer's spiritual maturity.

"**That Christ may dwell in your hearts by faith; that ye, being rooted and grounded in love, May be able to comprehend with all saints what is the breadth, and length, and depth, and height; And to know the love of Christ, which passeth knowledge, that ye might be filled with all the fullness of God.**" (Ephesians 3:17-19)

---

[49] Amos uses a "fourth" for emphasis. (Amos 1, 2)

This passage whetted my curiosity. Is there another mention of a fourth dimension? Then the passage in Revelation 21:6 surfaced. The *New Jerusalem* is described as being *four square.*

> "And the city lieth <u>foursquare</u>, and the length is as large as the breadth: and he measured the city with the reed, twelve thousand furlongs. The length and the breadth and the height of it are equal." (Revelation 21:16)

Could there be a fourth dimension in God's heaven? Mathematicians have built geometric systems around a fourth dimension, but it does not seem to exist in the reality that we know. Some day all believers will know the answer to this question. Another question: Will we really care? We will be in such awe of the Lord Jesus Christ that whether we live in a three, four, or seven dimensional heaven, this will be of little interest.

(3) Matter: The substance that makes up our perceivable material universe.

Matter, as currently perceived, is composed of three foundational substances; there are sub-particles and polymers but the three basics are: *atom, molecule, compound.* We considered each.

► **The Atom** consists of three basic particles: *proton, neutron, electron.*

The atom holds great energy. The energy formula was devised by Albert Einstein. It is a relationship triple:

$e = mc^2$ *Energy, Mass* of the atom, *Speed of Light.*

When God said, "**Let there be light**"—He enabled a calculation of the $e=mc^2$ relationship. This resultant energy is described as *atomic energy.*

A method for release of a tiny amount of mass to energy was tested in the 1940s. It resulted in the atomic bomb and nuclear reactors.

Question: How or where did the mass-energy of the universe originate?

The energy-mass input had to be monumentally colossal. How much? Simplistically stated: the total mass-energy potential of each atom is the sum of its nuclear binding energy, plus the binding energy of its electrons, plus the mass to energy ($E=mc^2$) *Energy.* For each atom in the universe—the mass-energy is individually colossal.

Next, think of this: there are an "innumerable" number of atoms that make up the totality of the universe with its billions of galaxies.

Then consider: for the *birth* of the universe, the *energy* input would need to be far more than an original "chunk" could contain or produce when it went "bang."

An omnipotent Creator was mandatory. God is omnipotent; His power (energy) is infinite. He created *(bara)*—by the "word of His power." Thus, at *creation*—all the mass-energy in the universe was *input* by God's almighty power, displaying "His eternal power and Godhead."

Humankind has made great knowledge breakthroughs and can even "blow up" lots of stuff with a single "boom." We even have learned how to synthesize life-saving chemicals that later contaminate the planet. It was these types of breakthroughs that some think God delayed by the Tower of Babel incident. God confounded the human language into many language families. It brought the potential expansion of knowledge to a standstill for more than four millennia.

Why the concern? It was not the height of the tower but the potential of a sinful, united human effort that could develop into a threat to the very existence of the human race. Are we at that point now?[50] As God viewed an unbridled human intent, He spoke to the point as He viewed the "tower" which was being built.

"And the LORD said, Behold, the people is one, and they have all one language; and this they begin to do: and now nothing will be restrained from them, which they have imagined to do. Go to, let us go down, and there confound their language, that they may not understand one another's speech.

So the LORD scattered them abroad from thence upon the face of all the earth: and they left off to build the city." (Genesis 11:6-8)

The *building* of the "tower" ended and so did any significant *increase* of human scientific knowledge—until now; knowledge expansion began about 400 years ago.

Question: Was this human potential to be totally terminated?

A passage in the Book of Daniel speaks to this: "But thou, O Daniel, shut up the words, and seal the book, even to the time

---

[50] What about human cloning? Humans stomped in moon dust and crashed some stuff on other planets, but could human cloning be invading God's reproductive design domain?

of the end: many shall run to and fro, and <u>knowledge</u> shall be increased" (Daniel 12:4).

Comment: It is evident that we live in a *time* in which knowledge is being *increased* and many are running "to and fro." If these passages in God's revelation have combined meaning, we are living in *the time of the end.* Human knowledge has exploded; technology has made life easier; but sin has not been abated.[51] When will God again "come down to see" and ultimately to judge? No one knows, but the world seems on the edge of self-destruction unless God intervenes again!

Back to the atom. By all the laws of nature, the atom should not be able to *hold together.* However, it does. Science has been trying to find the answer to the riddle. *The National Geographic,* (March 2008) ran a cover article, *The Hunt for the God Particle* (The Higgs Boson). The cyclotron in Switzerland was designed to help answer the question: What holds the atom together?[52] (Some phrase it: what gives the atom, mass?) Interestingly, Colossians speaks to this mystery. **"For by him *[Jesus Christ]* were all things created, that are in heaven, and that are in earth, visible and invisible, whether they be thrones, or dominions, or principalities, or powers: all things were created by him, and for him: And he is before all things, and by him all things <u>consist</u>"** (Colossians 1:16-17). (*Consist* means—hold together).

Note: The "God Particle" is really the Lord Jesus Christ, God Himself. He created all things and He continues to hold all *together.* To the believer Jesus has promised, **"I will never leave thee nor forsake thee."** This is the promise: Jesus Christ exercises *holding* power throughout the universe; He also *holds* His children—forever.

▶ **The Molecule:**

Molecules are made up of atoms with three basic kinds of bonds: Ionic, covalent, hydrophilic.

---

[51] A guru psychologist of 30 years ago spoke to the problem in his popular book. In summary, he indicated that a scientific method was needed to alter the nature of man. (B.F. Skinner, *Beyond Freedom and Dignity,* 1971)

[52] As this writing goes to publication, the news: "The particle has been found." *Questions*: Are they really sure? What is *its* holding power? However, a greater question: where did *it* originate?

► **The Compound:**

Atoms, molecules, and compounds exhibit properties that are in sets of *threes*:

- Magnitude, Mass, Weight
- Mass, Motion, Energy
- Solid, Liquid, Gas

TRIPLE—*[Bara]*

It was at this point that we disclosed a triple that is the key to the entire creation account. This *triple* in Genesis chapter one tells us that God *created* in *three* arenas or realms. The Hebrew word, create *[bara]*, is used for three realms.

God created the **cosmos** (1:1).

God created responsive animal **life** (1:21).

God created Adam and Eve "**In the image of God**" (1:27).

We will now look at this triple use of *create [bara]*.

(1) **God created** *[bara]* the perceivable **cosmos**: time, space, matter.

"In the beginning God <u>created</u> *[bara]* the heaven and the earth" (Genesis 1:1).

(2) **God created** *([bara]* animal **LIFE**.

"And God <u>created</u> *(bara)* great whales, and every living creature that moveth, . . ." (Genesis 1:21).

(3) **God created** *[bara]* man "***In the image of God.***"

"So God created man in his own <u>image</u>, in the <u>image</u> of God created he him; male and female created he them" (Genesis 1:27).

The triple use of the word *create [bara—to bring into existence from nothing]* refers to *three* unique acts of God's creative power. It also shows that those three *creations* were markedly diverse from each other.

(1) The **COSMOS**: This *bara* relates to the material universe in which we find ourselves.

(2) The **LIFE**: It was not the animals' bodies that were *bara*. It was the animal *life*.

But, what about *living* plants? For the plants, the statement, "**Let the earth bring forth**," does not claim to be a *creative* act.

Then we noted that there were *three* "Let . . . bring forth" statements: one for plants and two for the animals. This became the key to the entire concept of both the second and the third *create [bara]*.

For the animal kingdom, the *making* statements are, "waters *bring forth*," and "earth *bring forth*," indicating that the *body* material was not the *created* entity.

Yet in verse 21 is the second use of the word *create* as it related to the animal kingdom. The word *life* is used in verse 20 relating to animal **life**. We can only conclude that it was the **life** of the animal kingdom that was created *[bara]*. Thus, living plants and animal *life* are not the same *life* forms.

Also, for Adam, his body was "*formed* from the dust of the ground" indicating that the human body was also not the third *bara*. The *forming* account of Adam is recorded in Genesis 2:7 "And the LORD God formed man of the dust of the ground, and breathed into his nostrils the breath of life; and man became a living soul." The word create *[bara]* is not used for this *forming*.

This reveals two kinds of life forms: plant and animal.

Then we found two sets of repeats that were astonishing. For the plants, the term "after his kind" is a *triple*. But, the most astonishing part of the picture: "after his kind"[53] is repeated *seven* times for the animals. Thus, God makes another distinct difference between plant life and animal life because other passages clearly indicate that plant life was the provision for *sustainability* of both animals and humankind. Plants also help sustain the oxygen—CO_2 balance.

However, there is even a greater difference between animals and humanbeings. Animals and humans do have the common characteristics of *life* such as cellular structure including DNA, respiration, and reproduction. The creatures of the animal kingdom were *brought forth* and Adam's body was *formed*. Also, Eve's *body* was *made* from a rib of Adam [not *bara*].

Restated: animals were "brought forth" and both Adam and Eve were "formed." But the human uniqueness goes far beyond the body.

(3) The **IMAGE OF GOD**: It was the ***image of God*** in man that is the third unique *creation [bara]*. But what about Eve? Genesis 1:26, 27 also makes her *creation* issue triply clear and lists both male and female as being created in the *image of God*: "So God created man in his own image, in the image of God created he him; male and female created he them"

Both the man and the woman [male and female] were *created [bara]* in the ***image of God***.

---

[53] The NKJV uses the term: "according to its kind."

Question:

Consider the structure of a DNA molecule. How can the conjecture of evolutionary development explain its beginning and the continual replication of these molecules, each being unique to each living entity?[54]

MALE & FEMALE

We were amazed to find this as another truth that is *thrice trumpeted*. God created them:[55]

▶ "Male and female" (Genesis 1:27)

▶ "Fruitful and multiply" [male and female] (Genesis 1:28)

▶ "Male and female" (Genesis 5:2)

We could hardly imagine, another *triple* reference to *male and female*. But, there it was; this time in the New Testament. Two refer to marriage and one to equality.

▶ The first is Jesus speaking concerning the institution of marriage:
"And he *[Jesus]* answered and said unto them, Have ye not read, that he which made them at the beginning made them_ male and female. And said, For this cause shall a man leave father and mother, and shall cleave to his wife: and they twain shall be one flesh?" (Matthew 19:4, 5)

▶ The second record relates to the same occasion.[56]
"But from the beginning of the creation God made them male and female. For this cause shall a man leave his father and mother, and cleave to his wife; And they twain shall be

---

[54] "For the invisible things of him from the creation of the world are clearly seen, being understood by the things that are made, even his eternal power and Godhead; so that they are without excuse: Because that, when they knew God, they glorified him not as God, neither were thankful; but became vain in their imaginations, and their foolish heart was darkened. Professing themselves to be wise, they became fools." (Romans 1:20-22)

[55] The phrase, "male and female" as well as, "after his kind" is used numerous times in the Flood account (see *Appendix A*).

[56] These two passages reference the initial institution of marriage in Genesis 2:24. Thus, another *thrice trumpeted truth*: "leave and cleave."

one flesh: so then they are no more twain, but one flesh." (Mark 10:6-8)[57]

▶ The third reference is Paul speaking to the equality of male and female in God's salvation plan:

"There is neither Jew nor Greek, there is neither bond nor free, there is neither male nor female: for ye are all one in Christ Jesus" (Galatians 3:28).

Question:

Adam and Eve were created in the *image of God*. What are some human characteristics that reflect the Creator?

---

[57] These two passages clearly record Jesus' declaration that marriage unites a male and a female.

Section IV

The Image of God

Again, we ask the same question: "Are there any triply stated certainties related to the image of God in man? You already know the answer.

In Genesis 1:26, 27 God revealed His unique creative work for humankind and does it by a **dual triple** using the two words: *created* and *image*—referring to *the image of God*.

"And God said, Let us make man in our **image**, after our likeness: and let them have dominion over the fish of the sea, and over the fowl of the air, and over the cattle, and over all the earth, and over every creeping thing that creepeth upon the earth. So God <u>created</u> man in his own **image**, in the **image** of God <u>created</u> he him; male and female <u>created</u> he them."

The *triple* use of created and the *triple* image of God confirms a definite statement of *certainty*.

▶ "In our image" (Genesis 1:26)

▶ "Our own image" (Genesis 1:27)

▶ "Image of God" (Genesis 1:27)

God is clearly saying: "I CREATED *[bara]* humankind in the *image of God*."

This sets the creation of the human race apart from all other life forms. Human beings have a body as do animals; however, both male and female human beings were created in the unique *image of God*.

Questions:

▶ What could God have done or said to make the triple statement in Genesis 1:26, 27 more clear?

▶ Would three additional statements make it *more* clear???

To ignore the truth that God uniquely CREATED humankind can become a deliberate act of an individual's *will* that decides to *reject* God's revealed truth: "In the beginning God created."

Elihu stated: "Yet man perceiveth it not." What an indictment!

Peter said: "For this they willingly are ignorant . . ." (2 Peter 3:5).

THE IMAGE: *A Tripartite being*

God said He created humankind ("male and female") "in His own image."

Since God is Trinity, can we conclude that God created these first two people as tripartite beings? Thus our own human tri-being: body, soul, and spirit reflect God's three-in-one being. We found that there are three passages that list body, soul, spirit:

> **Isaiah** 26:9 "With my <u>soul</u> have I desired thee in the night; yea, with my <u>spirit</u> within me [<u>body</u>] will I seek thee early: for when thy judgments are in the earth, the inhabitants of the world will learn righteousness."

> **1 Thessalonians** 5:23 "And the very God of peace sanctify you wholly; and I pray God your whole <u>spirit</u> and <u>soul</u> and <u>body</u> be preserved blameless unto the coming of our Lord Jesus Christ."

> **Hebrews** 4:12 "For the word of God is quick, and powerful, and sharper than any twoedged sword, piercing even to the dividing asunder of <u>soul</u> and <u>spirit</u>, and of the <u>joints and marrow</u> *[body]*, and is a discerner of the thoughts and intents of the heart."

These three passages speak of the working of The Holy Spirit of God within the heart of His redeemed children. With our whole being, we are to seek after God. That is, with our body, soul, and spirit. Each displays a unique consciousness.[58]

(1) Body—*earth consciousness* using the human senses. Adam's body was formed from dust. His body was not created (*bara*). It was the "**image of God**" in man that was *created*. Most animal life also exhibits body senses, but humankind possess other unique abilities involving both soul and spirit. At death, the body returns to *dust* but the spirit returns to God who gave it.[59]

---

[58] There are passages that seem to use soul and spirit interchangeably. However, the three listed indicate a tri-partite being. Three should be a sufficient certainty.

[59] "All go unto one place; all are of the dust, and all turn to dust again." (Ecclesiastes 3:20)

"Then shall the dust return to the earth as it was: and the spirit shall return unto God who gave it." (Ecclesiastes 12:7)

Paul stated: "We are confident, I say, and willing rather to be absent from the body, and to be present with the Lord." (2 Corinthians 5:8)

All bodies die, both animal and human. However, the resurrection of the human body is clearly taught in the Scriptures. Resurrected bodies will stand at the judgments (1 Corinthians 15:10, Revelation 20:11-15). Also note, resurrected bodies will be different from our current atom/molecule bodies (1 Corinthians 15:42). Those who think "ashes" cannot be resurrected miss the point of a "new" body. Job spoke to the point: **"And though after my skin worms destroy this body, yet in my flesh shall I see God"** (Job 19:26).

Note: Meanwhile, at the *new birth* our bodies are indwelt by the Holy Spirit. Our bodies are then defined as "the temple of God." Paul speaks *four* times to that point: **"Know ye not that ye are the <u>temple</u> of God, and that the Spirit of God dwelleth in you? If any man defile the <u>temple</u> of God, him shall God destroy; for the <u>temple</u> of God is holy, which temple ye are"** (1 Corinthians 3:16-17).

In a following chapter Paul gives a clear commentary stating the temple is our body: **"What? know ye not that your body is the <u>temple</u> of the Holy Ghost which is in you, which ye have of God, and ye are not your own? For ye are bought with a price: therefore glorify God in your body, and in your spirit, which are God's"** (1 Corinthians 6:19-20).

(2) Soul—*self consciousness*: intellect, emotion, consciousness.

Note: Claims are made that animals exhibit emotion and/or will, yet none exhibit ability to reason. Studies have shown that dogs, apes, and elephants can solve simple problems. However, such problem solving is limited. None can use logical reasoning, language, read, write or do advanced mathematical computation. Birds build nests, but they do not manufacture building materials from raw elements. Only humankind was created "in the image of God" with added faculties.

(3) Spirit—*God consciousness*: a desire to know God and the spiritual dimension. It is the spirit of the person that will never cease to exist.

Note: Religious beliefs permeate all cultures. Even atheists and agnostics evidence a spiritual consciousness, often demonstrated by their preoccupation with ridiculing or even fighting against any kind of belief in the God of creation. Some even attempt to indoctrinate following generations. (Why not allow a free flow of ideas?) If there is no God, why not ignore "the idea" of a god completely? Many seem unable to ignore God, His message, or His messengers.

Conclusion: We are to seek the Lord with all our entire being. David described his own heart attitude toward God: **"As the hart *[a deer]***

panteth after the water brooks, so panteth my soul after thee, O God. My soul thirsteth for God, for the living God: when shall I come and appear before God" (Psalm 42:1-2)?

Problem questions:

If God created all things, including humans:

- Could God have some specific expectations for His creation?
- Could God's multiplicity of conservation laws indicate His desire for the sustainability of our habitat? (See Leviticus, Numbers, Deuteronomy).
- Could the "dominion" statements in Genesis 1:26, 28 and the "dress and keep" of Genesis 2:15 indicate His desire for sustainability?
- Could a person be accountable for the stewardship of him/herself, the other creatures and of the total *garden*?

Solution: In order to avoid any possibility of accountability for human action, the conjecture of *organic evolution* [the *origin* of life and replicating DNA molecules], allows one to bury the mind and reason in the sand. The eyes are blinded, but the whole person remains exposed and will be brought into judgment.[60]

Question: What are some special God-given abilities that enable humans to live within the created reality?

Interestingly, some of these abilities seem to flow from the fact that humanity is *uniquely* created in *the image of God.*

THE IMAGE: *A Human Mind*

Human intellectual ability is unique. The human brain and nervous system are similar to many animals. The neurons and synapses are not unlike some animals. What is different? It is obviously the *image of God* in humankind that provides a unique *imparting* of the human *mind*. Humans possess ability to observe, learn, make connections of information or devise a

---

[60] Proverbs 5:21-23 "For the ways of man are before the eyes of the LORD, and he *[God]* pondereth all his *[man's]* goings. His own iniquities shall take the wicked himself, and he shall be holden with the cords of his sins. He shall die without instruction; and in the greatness of his folly he shall go astray."

Ecclesiastes 12:13-14 "Let us hear the conclusion of the whole matter: Fear God, and keep his commandments: for this is the whole duty of man. For God shall bring every work into judgment, with every secret thing, whether it be good, or whether it be evil."

usable paradigm. The mind also exhibits creative ability and problem solving, but even more significant are the conscience and emotions such as love or empathy for other people.

Before we look at three unique *abilities*, we must ask the question: was/ is the image of God marred by the *fall into sin*? Some use the illustration of a mirror reflecting the image. If the mirror is shattered, it no longer produces an accurate or adequate reflection.

We found three specific passages that speak of the current state of the human *mind*.

▶ "And even as they did not like to retain God in their knowledge, God gave them over to a reprobate <u>mind</u>, to do those things *[wicked deeds]* which are not convenient." (Romans 1:28

▶ "But if our gospel be hid, it is hid to them that are lost:
In whom the god of this world hath blinded the <u>minds</u> of them which believe not, lest the light of the glorious gospel of Christ, who is the image of God, should shine unto them." (2 Corinthians 4:3-4)

▶ "This I say therefore, and testify in the Lord, that ye henceforth walk not as other Gentiles walk, in the vanity of their <u>mind</u>, ..." (Ephesians 4:17)

Paul continues the description of the current human condition.

"Having the <u>understanding</u> darkened, being alienated from the life of God through the ignorance that is in them, because of the <u>blindness</u> of their heart:
Who being <u>past feeling</u> have given themselves over unto lasciviousness, to work all uncleanness with <u>greediness</u>." (Ephesians 4:18,19)

From these passages, it becomes obvious that the *image of God* was/is significantly shattered. Have we ever noticed that the human mind is plagued with greed? TV commercials target human greed!

We like to think that our modern, sophisticated abilities are colossal. But we can only imagine the perfection, brilliance and keenness of Adam's and Eve's minds and intellect before their deliberate act of disobedience, especially their being "in tune" with God.

What abilities does the mind exhibit? Here are three that are definitely unique to mankind: *language, reason/logic* and *will.*

(1) Language: God communicated via language—He spoke with Adam, Abraham, Job, Elijah, Isaiah, Jeremiah and His disciples.

God created humankind with the ability of language. Language is rooted in intellectual abilities. Animals do not display significant linguistic skills. Some do evidence minimal communicative ability—but not language. Language requires several *triads* that animal "language" does not exhibit.

- Language: phonemes, words, syntax.
- The simple syntactic sentence: subject, verb, object.
- Three persons: first, second, third. (I, me; you; he/she)
- Communication is a triad: sender, message, receiver.

(2) Reason and logic: God spoke to our reasoning ability when He said, **"Come now, and let us reason together, saith the LORD: though your sins be as scarlet, they shall be as white as snow; though they be red like crimson, they shall be as wool" (Isa. 1:18).**

(3) Will: God gave man a freedom of choice—*a will.* (There are limitations).

It is interesting to note that most choices are *will* generated and have consequences. Isaiah spoke to that point: **"If ye be willing and obedient, ye shall eat the good of the land" (Isaiah 1:19).**

Here are three passages in which the writer states his own *willful* intent. **"But as for me, I will come into thy house in the multitude of thy mercy:" (Psalm 5:7)**

"I will keep thy statutes: O forsake me not utterly." (Psalm 119:8)

"And I will delight myself in thy commandments, which I have loved." (Psalm 119:47)

Sinful Behavior: Sinful behavior falls under the *will.* Each individual makes choices that are acts of the *will.* For humans to live harmoniously and happy, God gave a moral law—summarized in Ten Commandments. To violate God's commandments requires a choice, an act of the *will.*

- The account of the human fall into sin, identifies a three-step process to disobedience. **"And when the woman saw that the tree was good for food, and that it was pleasant to the eyes, and a tree to be desired to make one wise, she took of the fruit thereof, and did eat, and gave also unto her husband with her; and he did eat." (Genesis 3:6)**

The three steps: Eve *saw, desired, took.* Eve was deceived but she *willed* to eat.[61]

---

[61]   I Timothy 2:4

Adam was *tempted, agreed, ate.* Adam was not deceived. He ate deliberately. He *willed* to eat.

- The plea of the Savior speaks to the solution for human sinfulness. It involves three imperatives: *come, take, learn.*

"Come unto me, all ye that labour and are heavy laden, and I will give you rest. Take my yoke upon you, and learn of me; for I am meek and lowly in heart: and ye shall find rest unto your souls. For my yoke is easy, and my burden is light." (Matthew 11:28-30)

Heeding these directives results in *rest.* This *rest* is a *new life* in Christ. The Apostle John completes the issue when he states: "He that hath the Son hath life; and he that hath not the Son of God hath not life" (1 John 5:12).

Questions:

▶ How can any individual's sinful *will* make godly choices?
Paul answers this plaguing dilemma: "For it is God which worketh in you both to will and to do of his good pleasure." (Philippians 2:13)

▶ Why do you think Solomon wrote this triple directive followed by a promise: "Trust in the LORD with all thine heart; and lean not unto thine own understanding. In all thy ways acknowledge him, and he shall direct thy paths" (Proverbs 3:5. 6)?

▶ Should the creation triples which trumpet the truth that God did, indeed create the heaven and the earth, "and all that in them is," cause us to want to worship Him?
The Psalmist proclaims a resounding, "Yes." For he said:
"I will praise thee; for I am fearfully and wonderfully made: marvellous are thy works; and that my soul knoweth right well" (Psalm 139:14).

▶ Should the *truths* concerning the creation of humankind cause us to trust His promises?
When Jeremiah was in prison, God sited His own creative power and then identified a threefold course related to His workings with Israel. Israel was to *call* and then God promised to *answer* and to *show* mighty things.

"Moreover the word of the LORD came unto Jeremiah the second time, while he was yet shut up in the court of the prison, saying,

Thus saith the LORD the maker thereof, the LORD that formed it, to establish it; the LORD is his name;

<u>Call</u> unto me, and I will <u>answer</u> thee, and <u>shew</u> thee great and mighty things, which thou knowest not." (Jeremiah 33:1-3)

Based on the reality of His creative work, God *trumpeted* His ability to show great and mighty things. It seems logical to conclude that if God can create the universe, life, and design our planet's sustainability, He can also answer the call of His children with great and mighty things.

Next we will look for triples that *trumpet* the most spectacular working that God has ever wrought: His provision of *redemption* for the fallen human race.

Part Three
Redemption

We knew that we must look at the biblical account of redemption to see how many thrice trumpeted truths we could find. We also knew that the Scriptures are focused on the redemption of humanity from the power and penalty of sin. God created mankind *in His own image*, but both Adam and Eve wanted more. Since that initial covetous thought, people have a lust for more—with the *more* often going outside God's established boundaries for human welfare.

What to do about the fallen human condition? That is the story of redemption. The Old Testament points toward the coming of the Redeemer. The New Testament records His arrival, multiple evidences of who He was, His rejection, death, burial, resurrection and the spread of the Gospel message.

Our original investigative adventure did not include Jesus birth. During preparation for this publication, one of our original group asked: "Are there any triples in the account of Jesus' birth?" We hadn't looked at that. There were three gifts—that's one, so there may be more. Let's check it out.

So the writing began. My thought, "The birth of Jesus is the beginning of the most important sequence of events in the history of the human race. If there is one triple, why not *seven?*" So I wrote—knowing only one triple—the gifts; then I wrote, "My conjecture: there are *seven* sets of triples in Jesus' birth account."

Challenge: Sure enough. I found *seven* sets! There might be more. Before reading further, try to find some of these sets, or at least three of them. The ones I found are all recorded in either Matthew 1:18-2:23 or Luke 1:5-2:39. If you found more than seven sets, I would be interested to know what you found. (http://www.3-truths.com)

Triple Questions

▶ How many angelic appearances are related to the birth of Jesus?

▶ How many dreams helped direct Joseph?

▶ How many years did Jesus minister?

▶ There were how many disciples?

▶ It is a multiple of what number?

Section I
The Birth
Of
Jesus Christ

The birth of Jesus Christ in the village of Bethlehem is the focal event in the history of humanity. It was foretold by prophets, by Old Testament symbolism, and by God Himself. History has used Christ's birth as the "midpoint" of time. Because of Jesus' birth, years are identified by B.C and A.D.[62]

The New Testament assures us that the birth of Jesus Christ was at the right time in history. **"But when the fulness of the time was come, God sent forth his Son, made of a woman, made under the law, To redeem them that were under the law, that we might receive the adoption of sons" (Galatians 4:4-5).** Is there a triple in this passage?

Since the coming of Jesus Christ to this earth was a unique miracle, we would think that at least three Gospels would record the event. But only Matthew and Luke provide the account; each adds significant information. Many sets of miracles are recorded by three gospels (see *The Authority of Jesus*). However, only Matthew and Luke include the birth account. Could it be that God is saying, "Yes, the birth of Jesus was a *definite* event but the trials, crucifixion and resurrection will be affirmed by all four writers." Thus, we concluded that these should be the focal events rather than the birth.

Jesus' birth is an historic certainty, even recognized by those who reject His deity (He is God). Jesus' birth was announced by angels, by a star and by wise men bearing three gifts.

Initial conjecture: **"There are *seven* sets of triples."** After finding seven, we noted God's obvious intent for the reader to know that the account is reliable. Are there more? Interesting question!

Question: Can you find at least five of these seven? (Jesus visit to Jerusalem at age 12 is not included).

---

[62] The use of BC (Before Christ) and AD (*Anno Domini*) dates to Dionysius Exiguus in 525 AD. Contemporary political correctness, in its effort to eliminate the significance of Jesus, now labels BC as *BCE* and AD as *CE*.

THREE ANGELIC ANNOUNCEMENTS

These three announcements are recorded by the Gospel writer, Luke. For two of the announcements, the angel Gabriel, is named. The third only states that the angel appeared and spoke.

(1) To Zacharias: Chronologically, the appearance of an angel *[Gabriel]* to Zacharias would be the first of three angelic announcements since John Baptist was about six months older than Jesus. Here is Luke's account:

> "And there appeared unto him *[Zacharias]* an angel *[Gabriel]* of the Lord standing on the right side of the altar of incense.
>
> And when Zacharias saw him, he was troubled, and fear fell upon him.
>
> But the angel said unto him, Fear not, Zacharias: for thy prayer is heard; and thy wife Elisabeth shall bear thee a son, and thou shalt call his name John.
>
> And thou shalt have joy and gladness; and many shall rejoice at his birth.
>
> For he shall be great in the sight of the Lord, and shall drink neither wine nor strong drink; and he shall be filled with the Holy Ghost, even from his mother's womb.
>
> And many of the children of Israel shall he turn to the Lord their God.
>
> And he shall go before him in the spirit and power of Elias, to turn the hearts of the fathers to the children, and the disobedient to the wisdom of the just; to make ready a people prepared for the Lord" (Luke 1:11-17).

Obviously, John was to be the forerunner for the appearance of Jesus of Nazareth as the promised Messiah. Jesus referred to John when He said, "For I say unto you, Among those that are born of women there is not a greater prophet than John the Baptist" (Luke 7:28).

John's ministry was probably quite brief, but his message was clear and effective: "In those days came John the Baptist, preaching in the wilderness of Judaea, And saying, Repent ye: for the kingdom of heaven is at hand. For this is he that was spoken of by the prophet Esaias, saying, The voice of one crying in the wilderness, Prepare ye the way of the Lord, make his paths straight" (Matthew 3:1-3).

(2) To Mary: The second angelic announcement was to Mary, also by Gabriel.

> "And in the sixth month the angel Gabriel[63] was sent from God unto a city of Galilee, named Nazareth, To a virgin espoused to a man whose name was Joseph, of the house of David; and the virgin's name was Mary.
>
> And the angel came in unto her, and said, Hail, thou that art highly favoured, the Lord is with thee: blessed art thou among women.
>
> And when she saw him, she was troubled at his saying, and cast in her mind what manner of salutation this should be.
>
> And the angel said unto her, Fear not, Mary: for thou hast found favour with God. And, behold, thou shalt conceive in thy womb, and bring forth a son, and shalt call his name JESUS." (Luke 1:26-31)

It is interesting to note that Mary seemed to realize what the angel was saying and she voiced her concerns to the angel.

> "Then said Mary unto the angel, How shall this be, seeing I know not a man?
>
> And the angel answered and said unto her, The Holy Ghost shall come upon thee, and the power of the Highest shall overshadow thee: therefore also that holy thing which shall be born of thee shall be called the Son of God." (Luke 1:34-35)

The birth of Jesus was to be a supernatural birth. He will be "**The Son of God.**"

Also note that it was Gabriel that carried messages to Daniel on two occasions (Daniel 8:16; 9:21). Many commentators identify Gabriel as "God's messenger." These angelic messages announcing the birth of the Messiah were messages that will resound throughout eternity.

(3) To Shepherds: The third angelic appearance was to shepherds, announcing the birth of Jesus. There was one unnamed angel, then a multitude of the heavenly host, praising God.

---

[63] Gabriel is named again in this second appearance to announce the coming of the Messiah. Could it be that his third appearance will be to sound the trumpet for Jesus Christ's second coming?

"And there were in the same country shepherds[64] abiding in the field, keeping watch over their flock by night.

And, lo, the angel of the Lord came upon them, and the glory of the Lord shone round about them: and they were sore afraid.

And the angel said unto them, Fear not: for, behold, I bring you good tidings of great joy, which shall be to all people. For unto you is born this day in the city of David a Saviour, which is Christ the Lord." (Luke 2:8-11)

THREE DREAMS

It was to Joseph that an angel appeared in three distinct *dreams*. These were recorded by Matthew. This angel is not named.

(1) The first message was that Joseph should take Mary as his wife, even though she was obviously pregnant.

"Then Joseph her husband, being a just man, and not willing to make her a publick example, was minded to put her away privily.

But while he thought on these things, behold, the angel of the Lord appeared unto him in a dream, saying, Joseph, thou son of David, fear not to take unto thee Mary thy wife: for that which is conceived in her is of the Holy Ghost. And she shall bring forth a son, and thou shalt call his name JESUS: for he shall save his people from their sins." (Matthew 1:19-21)

Joseph did take Mary—to Bethlehem. The order to go to Bethlehem was not given by angels, but was due to Caesar's census strategies. God's providence and timing reached to the highest governmental authority.

(2) The second angelic message to Joseph was a warning concerning Herod's plot to kill Jesus. Joseph was to take Mary and Jesus to Egypt.

". . . behold, the angel of the Lord appeareth to Joseph in a dream, saying, Arise, and take the young child and his mother, and flee into Egypt, and be thou there until I bring thee word: for Herod will seek the young child to destroy him.

---

[64] Some commentators have speculated that these could have been the Temple shepherds, shepherding the sacrificial lambs for the daily Temple offerings.

When he arose, he took the young child and his mother by night, and departed into Egypt." (Matthew 2:13-14)

(3) The final (third) message to Joseph instructed him to leave Egypt and return home.

"But when Herod was dead, behold, an angel of the Lord appeareth in a dream to Joseph in Egypt,

Saying, Arise, and take the young child and his mother, and go into the land of Israel: for they are dead which sought the young child's life.

And he arose, and took the young child and his mother, and came into the land of Israel." (Matthew 2:19-21)

They returned to the land of Israel, but rather than returning to Bethlehem, they journeyed farther north to their original home in Nazareth.

We might ask, "Why did an angel appear to Mary, but to Joseph—the appearances were described as dreams? Allow another conjecture: could it be that God is making a definite distinction between the biological mother and the adopting father? Joseph was recognized as Jesus' *father*, yet the people knew that Joseph was not the biological *father*.[65]

THREE PRAISES

Going back to the account of John's birth, we find Mary journeying to Zacharias' and Elisabeth's home. Upon her arrival, an awesome event is recorded: Mary entered the home and was greeted by Elisabeth, who was six months pregnant. Luke recorded the meeting.

"And Mary arose in those days, and went into the hill country with haste, into a city of Juda; And entered into the house of Zacharias, and saluted Elisabeth.

And it came to pass, that, when Elisabeth heard the salutation of Mary, the babe leaped in her womb; and Elisabeth was filled with the Holy Ghost:" (Luke 1:39-41)

---

[65] Joseph was recognized as Jesus' "father" when they said, "Is not this the carpenter's son" (Matthew 13:55)? Also, Joseph was recognized as NOT being Jesus' biological father evidence by this accusation: "Then said they to him, *[Jesus]* 'We be not born of fornication' *[like you were]*" (John 8:41).

(1) Elisabeth: It was at this point that Elisabeth shouted out her praise.

"And she spake out with a loud voice, and said,

Blessed art thou among women, and blessed is the fruit of thy womb.

And whence is this to me, that the mother of my Lord should come to me?

For, lo, as soon as the voice of thy salutation sounded in mine ears, the babe leaped in my womb for joy.

And blessed is she that believed: for there shall be a performance of those things which were told her from the Lord." (Luke 1:42-45)

Question: How did Elisabeth know that this was a meeting with the mother of the *Messiah*?

Gabriel's message[66] to Zachariah had included the statement, "And he shall go before him in the spirit and power of Elias." That was a quotation from the prophet Malachi, who stated that one in the power of *Elijah* would precede the coming of Messiah. Zachariah and Elisabeth knew the Scriptures and, no doubt, realized that John was that *Elijah*. The inference would have also been that Messiah was soon to arrive.

(2) Mary: The second praise was Mary's. After Elisabeth's praise, Mary sounds forth an eloquent, magnificent praise to the Lord. Traditionally, this is known as *The Magnificat*.

"And Mary said, My soul doth magnify the Lord,

And my spirit hath rejoiced in God my Saviour.

For he hath regarded the low estate of his handmaiden: for, behold, from henceforth all generations shall call me blessed.

For he that is mighty hath done to me great things; and holy is his name.

And his mercy is on them that fear him from generation to generation.

He hath shewed strength with his arm; he hath scattered the proud in the imagination of their hearts.

---

[66]   Luke 1:17

> He hath put down the mighty from their seats, and exalted them of low degree.
>
> He hath filled the hungry with good things; and the rich he hath sent empty away.
>
> He hath holpen his servant Israel, in remembrance of his mercy;
>
> As he spake to our fathers, to Abraham, and to his seed for ever." (Luke 1:46-55)

Mary's praise was all about God, her *Savior*. She was amazed that God would choose her to be the mother of the Messiah. Her final praise recognized God's mercy and the fact that God had spoken to Abraham and thus, through the written record, to his seed forever.

(3) Simeon: The third praise was spoken by Simeon when Joseph and Mary took Jesus to the Temple in Jerusalem to be circumcised.

> "And, behold, there was a man in Jerusalem, whose name was Simeon; and the same man was just and devout, waiting for the consolation of Israel: and the Holy Ghost was upon him. And it was revealed unto him by the Holy Ghost, that he should not see death, before he had seen the Lord's Christ." (Luke 2:25-26)

The Holy Spirit revealed to Simeon that this baby was the *Promised One*. He responded with both a praise and a prophecy.

> "Then took he him up in his arms, and blessed God, and said,
>
> Lord, now lettest thou thy servant depart in peace, according to thy word: For mine eyes have seen thy salvation, Which thou hast prepared before the face of all people;
>
> A light to lighten the Gentiles, and the glory of thy people Israel." (Luke 2:28-32)

Can we imagine Joseph's and Mary's amazement upon hearing those words? "Mine eyes have seen thy salvation." Simeon then proclaimed the mission of Messiah. Luke continues his account: "And Joseph and his mother marvelled at those things which were spoken of him. And Simeon blessed them, and said unto Mary his mother, Behold, this child is set for the fall and rising again of many in Israel; and for a sign which shall be spoken against; (Yea, a sword shall pierce through thy own soul also,) that the thoughts of many hearts may be revealed" (Luke 2:33-35).

Mary's soul would be pierced and the child would also be pierced.

These three praises stated the mission of both John and Jesus. The Gospels record the accounts of their ministries, including both acceptance and rejection. John was executed and Jesus was tried and crucified. Today, we find the messages being proclaimed with the same results, either acceptance or rejection, often with the messenger being persecuted.

Note: There is another praise recorded by Luke and was the only dual praise statement related to both Messiah and to John as the prophet who would go before to prepare the way. Zacharias' words reach out to the coming messianic presentation to Israel. Zacharias had been unable to speak from the time Gabriel appeared until the moment that Zacharias wrote the words: "His name is John." It was then that he burst forth with praise.

"And his mouth was opened immediately, and his tongue loosed, and he spake, and praised God." (Luke 1:64)

Blessed be the Lord God of Israel; for he hath visited and redeemed his people,

And hath raised up an horn of salvation for us in the house of his servant David;

As he spake by the mouth of his holy prophets, which have been since the world began:

That we should be saved from our enemies, and from the hand of all that hate us;

To perform the mercy promised to our fathers, and to remember his holy covenant;

The oath which he sware to our father Abraham,

That he would grant unto us, that we being delivered out of the hand of our enemies might serve him without fear,

In holiness and righteousness before him, all the days of our life.

And thou, child, shalt be called the prophet of the Highest: for thou shalt go before the face of the Lord to prepare his ways;

To give knowledge of salvation unto his people by the remission of their sins,

Through the tender mercy of our God; whereby the dayspring from on high hath visited us,

To give light to them that sit in darkness and in the shadow of death, to guide our feet into the way of peace." (Luke 1:68-79)

Questions:

- While these praises were unique to a special time and situation, should we not also be praising God continually for what He has done, is doing, and will do in the future?
- Can you think of three things that the Lord has done for you this week that deserve your praise?
- Why do you think that most of us do more asking than praising?
- Who were the people that God used to publically proclaim the arrival of Messiah?

PROCLAMATIONS OF ARRIVAL

Then we found three proclamations to the public: by shepherds, by Anna, and by the wise men. Commentators have expounded various reasons that God used these three to announce to the people. We will not venture any additional speculations.

(1) Shepherds: First, it was the shepherds who heard the angelic announcement. They immediately went to Bethlehem, found the baby, worshiped Him, and then told the residents of Bethlehem that Messiah had been born.

> "And they came with haste, and found Mary, and Joseph, and the babe lying in a manger.
>
> And when they had seen it, they made known abroad the saying which was told them concerning this child.
>
> And all they that heard it wondered at those things which were told them by the shepherds." (Luke 2:16-18)

It should be no surprise that the shepherds were anxious both to find the baby and to proclaim His birth. An angelic message and a direct encounter with the Messiah was a goad to action. They were the humble *trumpeters* who were ignored.[67] It seems evident that their message had little long-term effect because during His ministry, no one accused Jesus of being born in Bethlehem.

---

[67] "But God hath chosen the foolish things of the world to confound the wise; and God hath chosen the weak things of the world to confound the things which are mighty; And base things of the world, and things which are despised, hath God chosen, yea, and things which are not, to bring to nought things that are: That no flesh should glory in his presence." (1 Corinthians 1:27-29)

Questions:

► If Luke were not *inspired of God* and the account of Jesus' were simply a story written about a "great" man, why would a "made up story" include a stable, a manger, and shepherds?
(Consider Isaiah 53:1-3; Zachariah 9:9).

► Why do you think that so many people, even today, seem more interested in a messenger's credentials than in the message?

► Some speculate that these shepherds were caring for sheep that would be offered in the Temple worship. Why is that an interesting speculation?

(2) Anna: The next record of an announcement of Messiah's arrival was by a woman who spoke to a select group in Jerusalem, We are not told the effect of her message. For those times, we can imagine that a message by a woman was also ignored.

> "And there was one Anna, a prophetess, the daughter of Phanuel, of the tribe of Aser: she was of a great age, . . . which departed not from the temple, but served God with fastings and prayers night and day. And she coming in that instant gave thanks likewise unto the Lord, and spake of him to all them that looked for redemption in Jerusalem." (Luke 2:36-38)

She spoke to all them that were looking for Messiah. Evidently she and Simeon were not the only ones expecting Messiah's arrival. She told them that He had arrived. What did they do with the knowledge? The messenger was an old woman. She lacked societal credentials, but she was God's chosen messenger, proclaiming a *revealed* truth. Evidently the announcement did not make any significant impact on the culture.

(3) Wise Men: Third, it was the wise men from the East who entered Jerusalem, probably many months later, seeking the King. Their search set all Jerusalem on edge, especially Herod, who was known for his jealous rage against any threats to his reign.

> "Now when Jesus was born in Bethlehem of Judaea in the days of Herod the king, behold, there came wise men from the east to Jerusalem,
>
> Saying, Where is he that is born King of the Jews? for we have seen his star in the east, and are come to worship him.
>
> When Herod the king had heard these things, he was troubled, and all Jerusalem with him." (Matthew 2:1-3)

We would think that the chief religionists would want to follow up on this inquiry. Evidently not, because 30 years later, no one seemed to remember anything about a special baby being born in Bethlehem. They thought Jesus to be from Nazareth in Galilee. No one asked Him the simple question: "Where were you born?" They made an observation, reached a conclusion, and missed the *truth*!!! They said: "**Search, and look: for out of Galilee ariseth no prophet**" (John 7:52).

By saying, "search," they were referring to the Scriptures. They knew that Micah had stated that Messiah would be born in Bethlehem.[68]

Thus, there were *three* witnesses: one in Bethlehem and two in Jerusalem. Yet few seemed to have shown any interest and just 30 years later, no religionist seemed to remember. The learned scholars had missed the *truth*. It becomes a simple process to be focused on one's present status and to ignore the things that relate to eternity. All who were living successfully in 30AD have been dead and existing in eternity for nearly 2000 years. Most lived for 50 or 80 years with their accolades, but are now existing for thousands-millions of years, each forever reaping the result of ignoring God.

THREE GIFTS

The Wise Men from the East followed the star, ultimately to Bethlehem. Matthew, who frequently addresses Jesus' kingship and the kingdom, records these events:

> "**Now when Jesus was born in Bethlehem of Judaea in the days of Herod the king, behold, there came wise men from the east to Jerusalem,**
>
> **Saying, Where is he that is born King of the Jews? for we have seen his star in the east, and are come to worship him.**" **(Matthew 2:1, 2)**
>
> "**And when they were come into the house, they saw the young child with Mary his mother, and fell down, and worshipped him: and when they had opened their treasures, they presented unto him gifts; gold, and frankincense, and myrrh.**" **(Matthew 2:11)**

The three gifts of gold, frankincense and myrrh are viewed as symbolic by many Bible commentators.

---

[68] Micah 5:2

(1) Gold speaks of Jesus' royalty.

(2) Frankincense speaks of the fragrance of Jesus' life. In the Tabernacle, the altar of incense was to offer a perpetual pleasing aroma toward God.

(3) Myrrh was used as a healing agent, serving two functions, as an antiseptic and an analgesic (used today, as well). We note that the Old Testament prophet stated that the Messiah would rise with healing in His wings.[69]

Myrrh had a *third* use: it was used by the Egyptians for *embalming*, thus speaking of Jesus' impending death.

JESUS' NAME

This triple was both unexpected and amazing. The Scriptures make certain that we know that the name, *Jesus*, was God given. The name was announced by an angel to both Mary and Joseph. This left no doubt of the assigned name. Then, both Matthew and Luke confirm the name of Jesus. The Name was *triply* verified.

(1) Jesus: The angel first appeared to Mary and stated:

"And, behold, thou shalt conceive in thy womb, and bring forth a son, and shalt call his name JESUS" (Luke 1:31).

(2) Jesus: Next the angel came to Joseph in a dream and declared:

"And she shall bring forth a son, and thou shalt call his name JESUS: for he shall save his people from their sins" (Matthew 1:21).

(3) Jesus: Naming the baby. The fact that the baby was given the name Jesus is stated by both Matthew and Luke:

". . . and he called his name JESUS" (Matthew 1:25).

"And when eight days were accomplished for the circumcising of the child, his name was called JESUS, which was so named of the angel before he was conceived in the womb." (Luke 2:21)

Comment: The name Jesus is probably the most familiar name in the English language. It is reverenced by believers. It is profaned by ungodly people. Why?

---

[69] See the prophecy in Malachi 4:2. Jesus Himself claimed to fulfill prophecy when replying to John's disciples: "Tell him that the lame walk, the blind see, and lepers are cleansed" (Matthew 11:4-6).

Questions:

- When you hear the name Jesus, what are your thoughts?
- What were the titles (names of Messiah) that Isaiah listed? (Isaiah 9:6)
- Which of the names in Isaiah 9:6 do you find to be the most fascinating? Why?

THREE HOMES

Jesus' childhood was spent in three locations:

(1) Bethlehem: Jesus was born in Bethlehem.

(2) Egypt: Joseph, Mary and Jesus escaped Herod's evil intent by fleeing into Egypt.

(3) Nazareth: Upon their return from Egypt, they returned to Joseph's and Mary's original home in Nazareth. This remained His "home" until, as an adult, He was rejected in Nazareth and moved His "home" to Capernaum.[70]

Comment: Evidently, the specific geographical location of Jesus' life was not to be a significant issue. Could the Lord be saying that it is not the town where we live but our relationship with God Himself that is important? We who know the saving grace of the Lord Jesus Christ are promised His presence wherever we are.[71] Abraham did not receive a permanent earthly home. His "home" was future: **"For he looked for a city which hath foundations, whose builder and maker is God (Hebrews 11:10).**

Let us live in the presence of the Lord where we are now.

Questions:

- ▶ What facts concerning Jesus' birth do you find to be amazing?
- ▶ What can you do to help focus the celebration of Jesus birth on Jesus rather than on ourselves?
- ▶ In what ways can these seven sets of triples be used to help us consider the miracle of His birth and also the miracle of the *inspired* story line itself?

The birth of Jesus fulfilled three prophecies in Matthew 1 & 2:

- 1:23—virgin born, God incarnate,
- 2:6—born in Bethlehem,
- 2:15—Egyptian sojourn

---

[70] Matthew 4:13; Luke 4:14-32.

[71] "Lo, I am with you always." (Matthew 28:20)

Note: Some might want to add the triple relating to Jesus' "growth" recorded in Luke 2:52. (There might be some other similar triples that we did not identify).

Some Questions

These questions relate to *The Tabernacle in the Wilderness*. These findings were another amazing discovery in our search for triples. However, they are not included in this publication. The study was fascinating!

▶ How many kinds of non-linen materials were used as a covering for the Tabernacle?

▶ How many entrances were there?

▶ How many kinds metals were used?

▶ How many kinds of woods were used?

▶ Were the numbers of planks, sockets, etc., a multiple of a specific number?

For more commentary:
http://www.3-truths.com

Section II
Thrice Trumpeted Truths In The Gospels

What about the four gospels? Next we came to the question, are there any *thrice trumpeted truths* found in any of the gospels? By this time in our searches we assumed that we would find some. We found the triples to be too numerous to include all. Here are three. We identified these as being *decisive* Three identifications as *The Word*, three identifications as being *The Son of God*, and three signs of Jesus *deity*.

▶ ***The Word:*** Jesus the Christ, is referred to as ***The Word*** three times in a single verse.

"In the beginning was
- **the Word**, and
- **the Word** was with God, and
- **the Word** was God." (John 1:1)

Clearly *the Word* is identified as the Lord Jesus Christ by this statement: "And **the Word** was made flesh, and dwelt among us" (John 1:14).

▶ ***Three Witnesses:*** We found three witnesses who testified that Jesus is the *Son of God* in The Book of John.

    ▶ **John the Baptist:** "And I saw, and bare record that this is the Son of God" (John 1:34).

    ▶ **Jesus, Himself:** "He said unto him, Dost thou believe on the Son of God? . . . And Jesus said unto him, Thou hast both seen him, and it is he that talketh with thee" (John 9:35-37).

    ▶ **John the Apostle:** "But these are written, that ye might believe that Jesus is the Christ, the Son of God; and that believing ye might have life through his name" (John 20:31).

▶ ***Three Signs:*** Here was another truth that we had not realized was a triple. Jesus was asked for a specific *sign* of His authority (*His deity*) on *three* occasions.

(1) In Jerusalem during Passover, Jesus cleansed the Temple. The religionists asked for a sign of His authority to do this. His response: "Destroy this temple, and in three days I will raise it up" (John 2:19).

John states that Jesus was referring to the temple of His body and His resurrection.

Then we saw another triple coming from that statement. Jesus originally announced this sign but it was later repeated by two other witnesses, making this *temple* sign a *thrice trumpeted truth* of Jesus' claim: "I will rise from the dead."

- Stated by Jesus (John 2:19).
- Quoted by witnesses at His trial (Matthew 26:61).
- Repeated by scoffers as He hung on the cross (Matthew 27:40).

The disciples did not realize the significance of Jesus' statement, but others did remember and quoted it as a foolish claim. The religionists also remembered, because they told Pilate of this prediction when they asked for a guard at the tomb.

The second and third of Jesus' *sign* statements were both *Jonah* signs with this same sign being stated on two occasions.

(2) The second sign referred the prophet Jonah. **"But he answered and said unto them, An evil and adulterous generation seeketh after a sign; and there shall no sign be given to it, but the sign of the prophet Jonas: For as Jonas was three days and three nights in the whale's belly; so shall the Son of man be three days and three nights in the heart of the earth"** (Matthew 12:39-40).

(3) The third pronouncement was a restatement of the *Jonah* sign some months later, also recorded by Matthew. **"A wicked and adulterous generation seeketh after a sign; and there shall no sign be given unto it, but the sign of the prophet Jonas. And he left them, and departed"** (Matthew 16:4).

Thus, another *thrice trumpeted truth* by which Jesus promised to rise from the dead. He promised a *resurrection* sign on three occasions. It was the resurrection that convinced His brothers and many of the priests (see John 7:2-5; Matthew 13:55, 56; Acts 1:13, 14; 6:7).

Section III
Who Is Jesus?

Did we find any triples in Jesus' claims about Himself? You already know the answer. Jesus claims and the evidences of His truthfulness are recorded by many statements.

While searching for triple repeats of Jesus' claims, our amazement was almost overwhelming as we identified the most frequently proclaimed title by Jesus: *Son of Man*. This was astounding! The title is recorded in the Gospels more than 80 times. Our conclusion: this is a **trumpeted truth**: Jesus was the prophesied *Son of Man*.

THE SON OF MAN

This phrase, *Son of Man* must have been extremely significant. Jesus defined Himself as "*the Son of man*" and is recorded more than 80 times in the four Gospels. Connected with most of these accounts, Jesus was describing or performing a *divine, non-human, miraculous* function. We can only conclude that the title does not refer to His humanity but to His being the *Messiah*. Here is one reference from each Gospel:

Matthew 9:6 "But that ye may know that the <u>Son of man</u> hath power on earth to forgive sins, ..."

Mark 2:28 "Therefore the <u>Son of man</u> is Lord also of the sabbath."

Luke 5:24 "But that ye may know that the <u>Son of man</u> hath power upon earth to forgive sins, (he said unto the sick of the palsy,) I say unto thee, Arise, and take up thy couch, and go into thine house." (See the entire passage: Luke 5:20-25).

John 1:51 "And he saith unto him, Verily, verily, I say unto you, Hereafter ye shall see heaven open, and the angels of God ascending and descending upon the <u>Son of man</u>."

If three repeats represent a *certainty*, 80 times should erase any question as to Jesus' claim.

This surprising count made us question: "Why was this phrase so frequently used and why was it so imposing to the religionists?"

The answer was found in the Old Testament. Actually the term, *son of man*, was used frequently in the Old Testament. For example: the Lord spoke to Ezekiel, calling him "son of man" more than 90 times. This referenced Ezekiel's *humanity*.

However, in one of his visions, Daniel identifies a unique *Son of Man* for all to recognize. Daniel's reference to *Son of Man* clearly refers to the *Messiah*. The religionists knew this reference and understood what Jesus was saying: He claimed to be the referenced "*Son of Man*." Daniel recorded his vision:

"I saw in the night visions, and,
behold, one like the <u>Son of man</u>
came with the clouds of heaven,
and came to the Ancient of days,
and they brought him near before him.
And there was given <u>him</u> dominion, and glory, and a kingdom,
that all people, nations, and languages, should serve him: his
dominion is an everlasting dominion,
which shall not pass away,
and his kingdom that which
shall not be destroyed" (Daniel 7:13, 14).

This passage does not speak of any normal man but clearly refers to *The Messiah*. Jesus, by defining Himself as *The Son of Man*, was definitely identifying Himself as *The Messiah*.[72]

Note: It is also evident that the *Son of Man* was not the identical personage as the *Ancient of Days* (God the Father).

Questions:

- If Jesus had been identified as *The Son of Man* three more times, would it have helped more to believe?
- If God would have said, "In the beginning God created the heaven and the earth," three more times, would that have helped more to believe? Actually, there are numerous references to creation in the Psalms and throughout the Scriptures.
- If Jesus would have said, "Come unto me all ye that labor and are heavy laden" three more times, would that help more people to believe?

---

[72]   The passage in Revelation 1:12-18 also identifies the *Son of Man.*

THREE TRIPLES

Then we found three triples that help answer the question: Who is Jesus? There are a multitude of statements concerning the Messiah and Jesus as to who He is and what He is. Here are three.

JESUS: the *"I am."*

When Moses asked who God was and who he should say sent him to deliver Israel, God identified Himself: "**I AM, that I AM**" (Exodus 3:14). Jesus made the same statement about Himself three times in John Chapter 8.

Note: In the following passages, the word *"he"* was added by the translators for what they thought was clarity. Jesus actually said, "**I am**" and the hearers knew that His *thrice* stated "**I am**" was a claim to both Deity and Messiahship. If they didn't hear it the first time, it was thrice stated. The *third* statement was such a forceful certainty that they tried to kill Him.

- "**I am** *he*"[75] John 8:24 "I said therefore unto you, that ye shall die in your sins: for if ye believe not that <u>I am</u> *he*, ye shall die in your sins."
- **I am** *he*"[75] John 8:28 "Then said Jesus unto them, When ye have lifted up the Son of man, then shall ye know that <u>I am</u> *he*, and that I do nothing of myself; but as my Father hath taught me, I speak these things."
- **I AM**" John 8:58 "Jesus said unto them, Verily, verily, I say unto you, Before Abraham was, <u>I am</u>."

John Chapter 18: (These passages will be referenced in Section V).

- "**I am** *he*" (John 18:5).
- "**I am** *he*" (John 18:6).
- "**I AM**" (John 18: 8).

See also Mark 14:62 and Luke 22:10.

JESUS: the *Light of the World.*

This is another *thrice trumpeted truth*, because Jesus stated this on three separate occasions in the Gospel of John.

- "Then spake Jesus again unto them, saying, I am the light of the world: he that followeth me shall not walk in darkness, but shall have the light of life." (John 8:12)
- "As long as I am in the world, I am the light of the world." (John 9:5)

- "I am come a light into the world, that whosoever believeth on me should not abide in darkness." (John 12:46)

The Light is a reference to Jesus' unique ministry of bringing light to all who heard him and to all who will hear Him. John clearly identified Jesus as being *The Light*.[73] "That *[Jesus]* was the true Light, which lighteth every man that cometh into the world" (John 1:9).

John, in his First Epistle, proclaims a truth concerning God's very being as *Light*, and relates this to Jesus. "This then is the message which we have heard of him *[Jesus]*, and declare unto you, that God is light, and in him is no darkness at all" (1 John 1:5).

This passage and others in First John, clearly indicate that Jesus Christ is *Light*.

Question: In what ways do the Scripture provide a "light unto my path" (Psalm 119:105)?

JESUS: the *Lamb of God.*

Jesus Christ was sent to be the ultimate sacrifice for sin. It is John's Gospel that records two references to Jesus as *"The Lamb of God."* John Baptist's testimony (twice stated).

- ▶ "The next day John seeth Jesus coming unto him, and saith, <u>Behold</u> the Lamb of God which taketh away the sin of the world." (John 1:29)
- ▶ "And *[John Baptist]* looking upon Jesus as he walked, he saith, <u>Behold</u> the Lamb of God." (John 1:36)

There is not a third, *"Behold* the Lamb of God."[74] *Question:* Will there be a *third* in the future? Could it be that the third will be *our* proclamation, *"Worthy* is the Ltamb that was slain"? (See Revelation 5:12).

Consider this: Could the High Priest's testimony be a third reference to *The Lamb of God*? The High Priest, Caiaphas, referenced someone *(a Lamb?)* dying for the people when he said,

---

[73] The prophet, Isaiah foretold that a great light would be seen. This was referenced in Matthew: "The people which sat in darkness saw great light; and to them which sat in the region and shadow of death <u>light</u> is sprung up" (Matthew 4:16)

[74] None of the references to *The Lamb* in Revelation is a "Behold" statement.

▶ "Nor consider that it is expedient for us, that one <u>man</u> should die for the people, and that the whole nation perish not.

And this spake he not of himself: but being high priest that year, he prophesied that Jesus should die for that nation; And not for that nation only, but that also he should gather together in one the children of God that were scattered abroad.

Then from that day forth they took counsel together for to put him to death" (John 11:50-53).

Thus the High Priest prophesied that Jesus should die. His crucifixion took place about two weeks later, at Passover, when Jesus became the final sacrifice as the Lamb of God.[75]

GOD: *The Trinity Manifest*

During the three years of Jesus ministry, there were *three* occasions in which God was manifest as Father, Son, and Holy Spirit.

▶ **At Jesus' Baptism:** (Matthew 3:16).

▶ **At the Transfiguration:** (Matthew 17:4-5).

▶ **At the Temple** during His final week (John 12:27-33).

(See *The Trinity Manifest*).

Questions:

▶ Can you think of any Old Testament hints of God's triune nature? How about Genesis 1:27; Genesis 11:7; Isaiah 42:1?

▶ Did Jesus meet the prophets' criteria at His coming? The prophet Micah, stated that Messiah's birth would be in Bethlehem. Bethlehem as Jesus' birthplace is stated three times by Matthew 2:1; 2:5; 2:8. In this eight verse passage Bethlehem is mentioned *three* times. Would His birthplace have been more certain if Matthew would have stated it a forth time? (See *Jesus' Birth*).

---

[75] "Forasmuch as ye know that ye were not redeemed with corruptible things, as silver and gold, from your vain conversation received by tradition from your fathers; But with the precious blood of Christ, as of <u>a lamb</u> without blemish and without spot: Who verily was foreordained before the foundation of the world, but was manifest in these last times for you." (1 Peter 1:18-20)

▶ What else do you think the Lord Jesus could have done or said to convince the religious leaders of His being the promised Messiah or of His divine mission?

▶ Could it have been possible that some did realize the reality of His claims because of the miracles and His fulfillment of the *Temple* and *Jonah* signs?

See John 12:42 and note in Acts 6:7 we read: "And the word of God increased; and the number of the disciples multiplied in Jerusalem greatly; and a great company of the priests were obedient to the faith."

Section IV
Jesus' Authority

Trumpeted in Three Gospels

It seems that several sections begin with a statement of amazement. Please do not tire of it. Remember our search was to last for 3 or 4 sessions because we did not realize that there were sufficient threes or triples for any type of prolonged study. This next section was discovered by accident and we were awestruck. Perhaps some readers had put these accounts together as triples of certainty, but I had not and neither had I heard nor read of these connections.

This was astonishing! We found *seven*[76] domains of Jesus' authority that are verified by a miracle or statement by Jesus with at least one incident for each domain being recorded in *all three* synoptic Gospels. These domains: authority over nature, over sickness, over blindness, over Satan, over the Sabbath, over the power of sin's penalty, and most significantly—over *death*. Each prove Jesus' claim to being the promised Messiah. Also note, a total of *twelve* of the following accounts are found in all three gospels.

(1) JESUS: *authority over Nature*

Here are *two* evidences, each being recorded in all three gospels.

▶ **The Storm is Stilled:** Recorded in three gospels.

- **Matthew** 8:23-27 "And when he was entered into a ship, his disciples followed him. And, behold, there arose a great tempest in the sea, insomuch that the ship was covered with the waves: but he was asleep.

  And his disciples came to him, and awoke him, saying, Lord, save us: we perish. And he saith unto them, Why are ye fearful, O ye of little faith? Then he arose, and rebuked the winds and the sea; and there was a great calm . . . .

  But the men marvelled, saying, What manner of man is this, that even the winds and the sea obey him!"

---

[76] We did not find eight. There may be more than seven, but any additional must be evidenced as the same event in each of the three Gospels.

- **Mark** 4:37-41
- **Luke** 8:24, 25 "Then he arose, and rebuked the wind and the raging of the water: and they ceased, and there was a calm.

  And he said unto them, Where is your faith? . . . And they being afraid wondered, saying one to another, What manner of man is this! for he commandeth even the winds and water, and they obey him?"

Questions:

- Are you experiencing any storms that create fear or doubt?
- In what ways does the Lord calm our storms today?
- Can you think of any storms that the Lord has calmed for you?

▶ **The Loaves are multiplied:** recorded in three gospels.
More tzhan 5000 were fed with a small amount of food.

- **Matthew** 14:13-21 ". . . And they say unto him, We have here but five loaves, and two fishes.

  He said, Bring them hither to me. And he commanded the multitude to sit down on the grass, and took the five loaves, and the two fishes, and looking up to heaven, he blessed, and brake, and gave the loaves to his disciples, and the disciples to the multitude.

  And they did all eat, and were filled: and they took up of the fragments that remained twelve baskets full. And they that had eaten were about five thousand men, beside women and children."
- **Mark** 6:34-43 ". . . And they did <u>all eat</u>, and were filled."
- **Luke** 9:13-17 ". . . And they <u>did eat</u>, and were all filled: and there was taken up of fragments that remained to them twelve baskets."

Questions:

- If we pray, "Give us this day our daily bread," in what ways does God supply our daily needs?
- God provided manna (Exodus 16:14, 15) for His people. Considering both the miracle of the manna and of the loaves—what spiritual lesson can we learn?
- Consider Jesus statement, "I am the bread of life." What "food" does He provide for us today?

(2) JESUS: *authority over sickness*

Jesus performed many miracles of healing, but we found *three* that are recorded in three gospels. Could it be that these have a special significance?

▶ **A leper is healed:**
- **Matthew** 8:2-4 "And, behold, there came a leper and worshipped him, saying, Lord, if thou wilt, thou canst make me clean. And Jesus put forth his hand, and touched him, saying, I will; be thou clean. And immediately his leprosy was cleansed."
- **Mark** 1:40-45
- **Luke** 5:12-16

▶ **Peter's mother in law is healed:**
- **Matthew** 8:14-17
- **Mark** 1:29-31
- **Luke** 4:38, 39 "And he arose out of the synagogue, and entered into Simon's house. And Simon's wife's mother was taken with a great fever; and they besought him for her.

    And he stood over her, and rebuked the fever; and it left her: and immediately she arose and ministered unto them."

▶ **A paralytic is healed:** these three passages will be referenced concerning Jesus' authority over sin.
- **Matthew** 9:2-8
- **Mark** 2:1-12
- **Luke** 5:17-26

Questions:

▶ Why do you think Jesus did not heal everyone in the whole nation? (See Mark 6:1-6)

▶ What did Jesus' miracles reveal about Him and in what ways is God glorified by a miracle?

▶ What is the greatest miracle?

▶ What miracle has the Lord Jesus Christ performed for you?

▶ What would it mean to pray: "Lord that I may receive my sight?

(3) JESUS: *authority over sight*

There are three accounts of the blind receiving their sight.[77] Each is mentioned in at least one gospel. However, the account of Jesus giving sight to the blind near Jericho is uniquely significant. It is recorded in three gospels and is the final of the three recorded *sight* miracles.

- **Matthew** 20:29-34 ". . . And, behold, two blind men sitting by the way side, when they heard that Jesus passed by, cried out, saying, Have mercy on us, O Lord, thou <u>Son of David</u>."

The two men asked for mercy, recognizing Jesus as *Lord*, and most importantly, recognizing Him as *Son of David* (Messiah).

- **Mark** 10:46-52 Mark names one of the men as Bartimaeus. Son of David (Messiah) is stated twice and is emphatic. ". . . he began to cry out, and say, Jesus, thou <u>Son of David</u>, have mercy on me. And many charged him that he should hold his peace: but he cried the more a great deal, Thou <u>Son of David</u>, have mercy on me."

Jesus recognized "FAITH" and stated: ". . . thy <u>faith</u> hath made thee whole." However, we must remember that it was Jesus who gave the sight; the "faith" was in Jesus ability to give sight. It was not the "faith" of the blind men that gave sight—it was Jesus!

- **Luke** 18:35-43 Luke's account records the same qualities as in Matthew and Luke but adds the report of one giving thanks. "And immediately he received his sight, and followed him, <u>glorifying God</u>: and all the people, when they saw it, gave praise unto God.

It should be noted that both Mark and Luke mention only one, rather than the two men in Matthew. Could it be that only Bartimaeus expressed thankfulness by following Jesus?

Comment: These men asked for mercy, recognized Jesus as "Son of David" (Messiah), demonstrated faith, and at least one followed Jesus. The result: the blind received sight and God was glorified.

The Lord came to "open the eyes of the blind." Anyone who will come with the same prayer as the blind men can receive spiritual *sight*.

---

[77] Jesus performed many miracles that are not specifically identified. Luke speaks to that point: "And in that same hour he cured many of their infirmities and plagues, and of evil spirits; and unto many that were blind he gave sight" (Luke 7:21).

Questions:

▶ Let us ask ourselves: Am I like the one who gave God praise for His working in my life or am I like the one who received a great miracle but gave no consistent praise for that miracle?

▶ Have your spiritual eyes been opened to see Jesus as your Savior?

▶ Can you think of three blessings that the Lord has provided to you in the past three days?

(4) JESUS: *authority over Satan*
and his demons/evil spirits.

Jesus demonstrated this authority on numerous occasions, two specific events being recorded in three gospels.

▶ **A Demoniac Healed:**

  • **Matthew** 8: 28-34 "And when he was come to the other side into the country of the Gergesenes, there met him two possessed with devils, coming out of the tombs, exceeding fierce, so that no man might pass by that way.

  And, behold, they cried out, saying, What have we to do with thee, Jesus, thou Son of God? art thou come hither to torment us before the time?

  And there was a good way off from them an herd of many swine feeding. So the devils besought him, saying, If thou cast us out, suffer us to go away into the herd of swine.

  And he said unto them, Go.

  And when they were come out, they went into the herd of swine: and, behold, the whole herd of swine ran violently down a steep place into the sea, and perished in the waters, ..."

  • **Mark** 5:1-20 ". . . For he said unto him, Come out of the man, thou unclean spirit."

  • **Luke** 8:26-39 ". . . Then went the devils out of the man, and entered into the swine: and the herd ran violently down a steep place into the lake, and were choked.

▶ **Demons are cast out of a boy:**

Jesus used this occasion to teach concerning believing God and an open-ended promise to anyone who does *believe*.

  • **Matthew** 17:14-18

  • **Mark** 9:17-27 "Jesus said unto him, If thou canst believe, all things are possible to him that believeth.

And straightway the father of the child cried out, and said with tears, Lord, I believe; help thou mine unbelief . . . . But Jesus took him by the hand, and lifted him up; and he arose."

- **Luke** 9:38-42

Comment: The Apostle Peter states that it is faith that *resists* and has authority over the devil's attacks. "Casting all your care upon him; for he careth for you. Be sober, be vigilant; because your adversary the devil, as a roaring lion, walketh about, seeking whom he may devour: Whom <u>resist</u> stedfast in the faith" (1 Peter 5:7-9).

The faith must be in Jesus Christ. Our *faith* is not the authority. Many people seem to think that their "faith" must be in their *faith*. However, the *authority* is Jesus Christ and our faith is in *His authority* and His abilities, not in *our* ability to generate some kind of "faith."

Faith is a gift from God—it is not of our generation: see Ephesians 2:8. Also consider this passage: "For it is God which worketh in you both to will and to do of his good pleasure" (Philippians 2:13).

Questions:

▶ Is the picture beginning to focus?
The fact that a truth is stated three times should be sufficient for us to all rejoice together in Jesus Christ's past, present, and future authority. We can be triply certain of Jesus' authority.

▶ Let us ask ourselves: "Am I like the one who gives God praise for His working?

▶ Might it be wise for believers to pray, "Help mine unbelief" (Mark 9:24)?

(5) JESUS: *authority over the Sabbath*

The Sabbath, the seventh day of the week was to be a special day. It had been defined in Moses' Law as a day in which NO work was to be done. It should also be noted that some other holy days were also defined as Sabbath days. Jesus *thrice* stated that He was "Lord, even of the Sabbath."

- **Matthew** 12:8 "For the Son of man is Lord even of the sabbath day."
- **Mark** 2:28 "Therefore the Son of man is Lord also of the sabbath."
- **Luke** 6:5 "That the Son of man is Lord also of the sabbath."

These were claims of being superior to Moses. The religionists could also interpret it as claiming equality with God.

The Gospels provide three individual records of Jesus healing on the Sabbath. Each account records an encounter with the religionists who questioned His "working" on the Sabbath.

- **Luke** 13:10-17 A woman was healed on the Sabbath.
- **Luke** 14:2-6 A man with dropsy was healed on the Sabbath.
- **John** 5:1-16 The man at the Pool of Bethesda was healed on the Sabbath.

We noted that Jesus healed the sick, not only to demonstrate His compassion, but also to prove that He was the Messiah.

The Sabbath was a very special day modeled by God (He rested on the seventh day) and later instituted in Moses' Law. To be **"Lord of the Sabbath"** was making claim to be "greater than Moses." Jesus' claim is triply trumpeted for all to note. His messianic claims were verified throughout His ministry.

But how about this? One specific event is recorded in three Gospels. Jesus healed the man with a withered hand—on the Sabbath.

- **Matthew** 12:9-13
- **Mark** 3:1-5
- **Luke** 6:6-11

(6) JESUS: *authority over sin's penalty*

▶ **The palsied man healed** (recorded in three gospels).
"Thy sins be forgiven thee" are words of divine authority.

- **Matthew** 9:2-8 "And, behold, they brought to him a man sick of the palsy, lying on a bed: and Jesus seeing their faith said unto the sick of the palsy; Son, be of good cheer; thy sins be forgiven thee."
- **Mark** 2:1-12 "When Jesus saw their faith, he said unto the sick of the palsy, Son, thy sins be forgiven thee."
- **Luke** 5:18-26 "And when he saw their faith, he said unto him, Man, thy **sins are forgiven thee** . . . . Whether is easier, to say, Thy sins be forgiven thee; or to say, Rise up and walk? But that ye may know that the Son of man hath power upon earth to forgive sins.

Questions:

▶ When a sinner comes to Jesus today, can he/she be assured that Jesus Christ has the authority to forgive sin?

▶ On what basis can an individual have his/her sins forgiven?

▶ To *repent* means to turn to God and away from sinning. If an individual does not *repent*, would he/she be truly asking for forgiveness?

(7) JESUS: *authority over Death*

Jesus raised three people from the dead. This is a *triple* that demonstrated the *certainty* of His power over death. The three miracles triply verified that He had the power to rise from the dead Himself. It is interesting to note that there were also three specific events of a resurrection in the Old Testament. Jesus Christ is making it clearly certain to mankind by demonstrating, "I have power over death."

▶ **The Widow's Son:**

As the account reads, it almost seems an "accident" that Jesus was in the area as they carried the body of a widow's son to be buried. This is the first of the *three* resurrection miracles.

> **Luke** 7:12-16 "And he came and touched the bier: and they that bare him stood still. And he said, Young man, I say unto thee, Arise. And he that was dead sat up, and began to speak. And he delivered him to his mother."

▶ **The Daughter of Jairus:**

Jairus was a ruler of the synagogue. Throughout the Gospels, most of the chief priests, rulers, Pharisees, and other religious leaders refused to acknowledge Jesus' authority.[78] Jairus, in desperation requests Jesus to heal his sick daughter. As Jesus was coming to the home, the daughter died. Jesus raised her to life. This is the second resurrection proof of His authority. This event is recorded in three Gospels.

- **Matthew** 9:23-26 "But when the people were put forth, he went in, and took her by the hand, and the maid arose. And the fame hereof went abroad into all that land."
- **Mark** 5:38-43.
- **Luke** 8:51-55.

---

[78] At least three did believe: Jairus, Nicodemus, Joseph of Arimathaea.

Jesus' authority over death was being established. He had been telling His disciples that He would suffer, die, and rise again. It was not that they doubted His ability, they witnessed it, but they "did not hear" what He was telling them. After His death, not one of the *disciples* went to the tomb with any expectation of His resurrection.

▶ **Lazarus:**

Mary, Martha, and Lazarus frequently hosted Jesus visits to the Jerusalem area. About two weeks before Jesus' triumphant entry into Jerusalem, news came that Lazarus was sick. Jesus waited until Lazarus had died before responding. The entire account is spectacular as Jesus says, **"Whosoever liveth and believeth in me shall never die."** Lazarus had died! Jesus authority over death was to be evidenced as *certain* by this *third* resurrection. John's account is clear.

> **John 11:14-44** "Then said Jesus unto them plainly, Lazarus is dead . . . .
>
> Jesus said unto her, I am the resurrection, and the life: he that believeth in me, though he were dead, yet shall he live: And whosoever liveth and believeth in me shall never die. Believest thou this?
>
> She saith unto him, Yea, Lord: I believe that thou art the Christ, the Son of God, which should come into the world . . . .
>
> And Jesus lifted up his eyes, and said, Father, I thank thee that thou hast heard me. And I knew that thou hearest me always: but because of the people which stand by I said it, that they may believe that thou hast sent me.
>
> And when he thus had spoken, he cried with a loud voice, Lazarus, come forth.
>
> And he that was dead came forth, bound hand and foot with graveclothes: and his face was bound about with a napkin. Jesus saith unto them, Loose him, and let him go."

This event evidenced the certainty that Jesus had power over death. But again we should note: after His death the disciples were not expecting an empty tomb. It was not until He showed Himself alive that they remembered His resurrection statements.

Note: The raising of Lazarus sealed Jesus' fate with the High Priest.[79]

Questions:

The religious leaders witnessed *three* years of miracles and even *three* persons being raised from the dead.

▶ Why do you think they were unwilling to recognize Jesus as being their Messiah?

▶ What was their root sin?

▶ Why do you think people today are unwilling to accept Jesus as being their Lord and Savior from sin?

Comment: As we proceeded through the months of search and find, it was amazing to see these triples not simply as a repeated literary structure, but also as affirmation of key scriptural truths and evidence that God's inspired writers "spake as they were moved by the Holy Spirit."[80]

---

[79] "And one of them, named Caiaphas, being the high priest that same year, said unto them, Ye know nothing at all, Nor consider that it is expedient for us, that one man should die for the people, and that the whole nation perish not. And this spake he not of himself: but being high priest that year, he prophesied that Jesus should die for that nation;" (John 11:49-51)

[80] 2 Peter 1:21

Section V
Jesus' Last Day

By now it should be evident: we were looking for triples in all types of settings. When our search for triples began to focus on Jesus' last 24 hours, amazingly they began to leap out at us. The events were the Passover supper, the garden agony, a religious trial, two political trials, His crucifixion, and death.

I had heard many messages based on these accounts, read commentaries, and consulted various authors, but none identified the multiple triples. Thus, it was a personal thrill to find these new insights into the certainty of God's revelation; there were so many that it cannot be a statistical accident. These patterns reflect an amazing, revealed design because we know that "**holy men spake as they were moved by the Holy Spirit.**" The Lord was so purposeful in His revelation that any reader must pause to ponder its awesomeness.

THE PASSOVER FEAST

Jesus celebrated the feast of the Passover with His disciples in the upper room. Three items were included in the account (Luke 22:14-22). In this account, Jesus:

- shared the first *cup*[81],
- broke the *bread*[82] and later
- declared the Passover *cup* to be "**The New Testament in my blood, which is shed for you**" (Luke 22:20).

Upon completion of the Passover Supper, He took the disciples to the Garden of Gethsemane, where He suffered tremendous physical, mental and spiritual agony as He anticipated His trials and their ignominy. However, the greatest agony would be taking upon Himself the sins of the world (yours and mine), and the ultimate torment: "**My God, My God, why hast thou forsaken me?**"

Matthew recorded Jesus' steadfast, forward march toward completion of His Father's plan of redemption: "**Then saith Jesus unto them, All ye**

---

[81] "Take this, and divide it among yourselves . . ." (Luke 22:17)

[82] "This is my body which is given for you: this do in remembrance of me." (Luke 22:19)

shall be offended because of me this night: for it is written, I will smite the shepherd, and the sheep of the flock shall be scattered abroad. But after I am risen again, I will go before you into Galilee . . . . Then saith he unto them, My soul is exceeding sorrowful, even unto death: tarry ye here, and watch with me" (Matthew 26:31-38).

JESUS' DEATH: *Voluntary*

The following passages, one from each of the four Gospels, is a fourfold declaration that Jesus knew His mission was to be completed by His death and resurrection.

Matthew 20:18 "Behold, we go up to Jerusalem; and the Son of man shall be betrayed unto the chief priests and unto the scribes, and they shall condemn him to death,"

Mark 10:33 "Saying, Behold, we go up to Jerusalem; and the Son of man shall be delivered unto the chief priests, and unto the scribes; and they shall condemn him to death, and shall deliver him to the Gentiles:"

Luke 18:32-33 "For he shall be delivered unto the Gentiles, and shall be mocked, and spitefully entreated, and spitted on: And they shall scourge him, and put him to death: and the third day he shall rise again."

John 10:17 "Therefore doth my Father love me, because I lay down my life, that I might take it again."

We found nine indicators (three sets of triples: a *certainty*) that show us that Jesus knew the outcome, that the "soldiers" had the right person and that Jesus surrendered willingly! These were three prayers, three identifications, and three statements by Jesus.

THREE PRAYERS

Matthew was especially clear in his account by recording *three* prayers stating Jesus' submission to the Father and His willingness to take upon Himself the sins of the whole world.

Three gospels record Jesus' agony in the garden and the three prayers.

Matthew 26:39-44 "And he went a little further, and fell on his face, and prayed, saying, O my Father, if it be possible, let this cup pass from me: nevertheless not as I will, but as thou wilt.

He went away again the second time, and prayed, saying, O my Father, if this cup may not pass away from me, except I drink it, thy will be done . . . .

And he left them, and went away again, and prayed the <u>third</u> time, saying the same words."

Mark 14:36-41; **Luke** 22:42-45

Question: Why three prayers?

Each expressed both agony and determination. Isaiah had foretold this determination: "The Lord GOD hath opened mine ear, and I was not rebellious, neither turned away back" (Isaiah 50:5).

THREE IDENTIFICATIONS

After Jesus prayed, Judas arrived with the mob. Even though the night was illuminated by a full moon, identification would have been uncertain because of the custom for men to wear a head-covering that partly obscured the facial features.

(1) Judas Identification of Jesus:

Judas knew the area and recognized Jesus' profile in the moon's light. He had agreed to betray Jesus for a fee: 30 pieces of silver.

"And he that betrayed him had given them a token, saying, Whomsoever I shall kiss, that same is he; take him, and lead him away safely.

And as soon as he was come, he goeth straightway to him, and saith, Master, master; and kissed him. (Mark 14:44-45)

(2) Jesus' Self Identification:

As the mob approached, John recorded an interesting dialogue: Jesus asked the mob, "Whom seek ye?"

The mob responded: "Jesus of Nazareth."

"Jesus saith unto them, "I am he."[83]

"As soon then as he had said unto them, I am he, they went backward, and fell to the ground" (John 18:4-6).

Jesus could have walked away as He had done earlier in His ministry.

Again, He asks, "Whom seek ye?

---

[83] The "*he*" is added by the translators for language flow clarity.

(3) Jesus' second Self Identification: "I have told you that "I am *he*" (John 18:8).

Interestingly, Jesus direct statement, "**I am** *he*" is only stated *twice*. But, since Judas had already made one positive identification, there were a total of three. It was *certain* that Jesus was the right person to seize.

Question: Will Jesus Himself make the *third* statement, "**I am** *he*" at His second coming?

> His spectacular appearance will boldly state: "**I AM.**" His appearance will also proclaim: "**I AM here, I have returned!**"
> Remember Jesus' final statement to Jerusalem: "For I say unto you, Ye shall not see me henceforth, till ye shall say, Blessed is he that cometh in the name of the Lord" (Matthew 23:39).
> Jesus Christ's triumphant return will awesomely proclaim: "I AM THAT I AM" (Exodus 3:14).

THREE STATEMENTS

When the mob confronted and captured Jesus, He addressed three statements to those around Him. Let's observe and listen.

(1) To Judas: "Friend, wherefore art thou come" (Matthew 26:50)?

> Vigilant Peter draws his sword and strikes a servant's ear.

(2) To Peter: "Put up again thy sword" (Matthew 26:52).

> The mob surrounds Jesus. Jesus speaks:

(3) To the Mob: "Are ye come out as against a thief with swords and staves for to take me? I sat daily with you teaching in the temple, and ye laid no hold on me" (Matthew 26:55).

> Matthew inserted a link from the Old Testament prophecy to the event: "But all this was done, that the scriptures of the prophets might be fulfilled" (Matthew 26:56).

> The disciple's reaction was also recorded by Matthew, a disciple: "Then all the disciples forsook him, and fled" (Matthew 26:56).

Section VI

Jesus' Trials

I knew it, but had never put the three trials together in my mind as having the significance of a *certain triple*. But here they were, three ruling jurisdictions, each declaring the death sentence of the Redeemer.

There have been trials of the century, but these were the trials of *the ages*. Some have said that Jesus' trials were a battle between *good* and *evil*, but they each go beyond a question of ethics. Each trial displayed powerful evidences of the continuing *battle* between God and Satan.

This battle can be described as **a *three* round battle.**

The Epic Battle
Three Rounds

ROUND ONE

The account of *round one* was revealed to the prophet Isaiah. Interestingly, as we looked at Satan's initial rebellion against God we found another unique number, *five* (5).[84] Satan proclaimed *five* defiant declarations of war. Satan declared: "I will," *five times.*

"How art thou fallen from heaven, O Lucifer, son of the morning! how art thou cut down to the ground, which didst weaken the nations! For thou hast said in thine heart, I will ascend into heaven, I will exalt my throne above the stars of God: I will sit also upon the mount of the congregation, in the sides of the north: I will ascend above the heights of the clouds; I will be like the most High." (Isaiah 14:12-14)

These *five* "I wills" continued to be Satan's battle cry during the three trials. However, God's initial response to Satan's *five* rebellious proclamations was a single pronouncement of Satan's final doom:[85] "Yet thou shalt be brought down to hell, to the sides of the pit" (Isaiah 14:15).

It was Jesus who testified: "I beheld Satan as lightning fall from heaven" (Luke 10:18).

---

[84] It is interesting to note that some "Satanic" symbols display *five* points or facets.

[85] The final blow to Satan's defiance is found in Revelation 20:10.

Questions:

▶ Is there any evidence that Satan and his demons continually attempt to hinder God's plans for His children?

▶ Has the history of mankind been effected by a continuation of this epic battle?

▶ Could any of the horrible things that seem to happen to people today be an indication of Satan's efforts to hinder God's Word and works from being known and followed?

Job's friends blamed both Job and God for the troubles. However, Job 1, 2 ascribe the trouble to *Satan.*

▶ What should be our response to temptation? (See Psalm 119:9-11).

ROUND TWO[86]

As Jesus began His ministry, Satan "tempted" (attacked) Him with *three* propositions as recorded by the apostle Matthew.

(1) The first attack was against Jesus as being the Son of God.
"And when the tempter came to him, he *[Satan]* said, If thou be the Son of God, command that these stones be made bread." (Matthew 4:3)

Jesus' response was to quote an Old Testament passage:[87] "But he *[Jesus]* answered and said, It is written, Man shall not live by bread alone, but by every word that proceedeth out of the mouth of God" (Mathew 4:7).

(2) The second attack also questioned Jesus' Sonship:

"Then the devil taketh him up into the holy city, and setteth him on a pinnacle of the temple, And saith unto him, If thou be the Son of God, cast thyself down: for it is written, He shall give his angels charge concerning thee: and in their hands they shall bear thee up, lest at any time thou dash thy foot against a stone." (Matthew 4:5, 6)

---

[86] On two previous occasions Satan had attempted to destroy the *royal* line for Messiah's birth. These three "temptations" were a direct attack, an attempt to destroy Jesus' divine mission.

[87] Deuteronomy 8:3

Jesus' second response was again to quote an Old Testament passage:[88]

> **"Jesus said unto him, It is written again, Thou shalt not tempt the Lord thy God." (Matthew 4:7)**

(3) The third attack was an offer for a shortcut to the Kingdom.

> **"Again, the devil taketh him up into an exceeding high mountain, and sheweth him all the kingdoms of the world, and the glory of them; And saith unto him, All these things will I give thee, if thou wilt fall down and worship me." (Matthew 4:8, 9)**

Jesus' third response was a triumphant rebuke: **"Then saith Jesus unto him, Get thee hence, Satan: for it is written, Thou shalt worship the Lord thy God, and him only shalt thou serve"**[89] **(Matthew 4:10).**

Jesus' rebuke was definite and effective: **"Then the devil leaveth him, and, behold, angels came and ministered unto him" (Matthew 4:11).**

Satan was unable to move Jesus from His determination to adhere to the written Word of God.

ROUND THREE

Did Satan really think this would be the final round? Jesus was taken captive by wicked men who were determined to kill Him. Little did they realize that their actions were like those of puppets in Satan's hands throughout *"round three"* of this continuing battle.

Again, we were amazed to find this account to be filled with triples.

Let's become spectators! Remember the series: "You are there"? In a sense, we were there as our sins were placed on Him![90]

What do we see? Jesus is in the custody of wicked men. The battle intensifies as three trials unfold. But notice, it is Jesus who willingly submits to the wickedness of evil men.

Is Satan in control and will he be able to fulfill his ultimate I WILL? A prophetic passage captures the drama: **"They gaped upon me with their mouths, as a ravening and a roaring lion" (Psalm 22:13).**

---

88 Deuteronomy 6:16

89 Deuteronomy 6:13; Exodus 20:3-5.

90 ". . . the LORD hath laid on him the iniquity of us all." (Isaiah 53:6)
"For he hath made him to be sin for us, who knew no sin; that we might be made the righteousness of God in him." (2 Corinthians 5:21)

Yet, we now know that each event, each action, the chants, the ridicule, the stripes, the *robe*, the *rod*, the *crown* and *the cross* were all within God's eternal plan for the redemption of mankind.

As we observe the three trials, they become an *ironic paradox.*

First, we see Satan's effort to defeat God's eternal purposes by encouraging wicked men to "kill" their Messiah.

Then, we discover that God's ultimate plan is being fulfilled.

The result: the redemption of mankind is being provided. The veil will be opened, and by faith we may enter into the very presence of God.

THREE QUESTIONS

Interestingly, as Jesus is ridiculed, mocked, and tortured, He responds to three basic questions:[91]

(1) Who are You?

This is the key question that all mankind must answer concerning Jesus. In each of the three trials, Jesus identity is investigated and His claim to being The Christ is clearly stated three times in each gospel account.

In each trial, we hear the "Who are you?" Jesus responds with a confirming proclamation: **"I AM** who I claim to be."

▶ **To Caiaphas.** (Recorded in three of the Gospels).
Matthew 26:63, 64 "And the high priest answered and said unto him, I adjure thee by the living God, that thou tell us whether thou be the Christ, the Son of God.
Jesus saith unto him, **Thou hast said**:"
Mark 14:61, 62 "But he held his peace, and answered nothing. Again the high priest asked him, and said unto him, Art thou the Christ, the Son of the Blessed? And Jesus said, **I am**:"
Luke 22:70 "Then said they all, Art thou then the Son of God? And he said unto them, Ye say that **I am**."

▶ **To the Council.** (Recorded in three of the Gospels).
Mark 14:62 "**I am**: and ye shall see . . ."
Luke 22:70 "Ye say that **I am**."

---

[91] "As a sheep before his schearers is dumb, so He *[Jesus]* opened not His mouth." (Isaiah 53:7)

John 18:19-23 (Jesus' full statement is recorded in this passage where He refers to His previous statements which would include His: "**I am**.")[92]

▶ **To Pilate.** (Recorded in three of the Gospels).
Matthew 27:11 "And Jesus stood before the governor: and the governor asked him, saying, Art thou the King of the Jews? And Jesus said unto him, Thou sayest."
Mark 15:2 "Thou sayest."
Luke 23:3 "Thou sayest it."

The Apostle John adds another aspect as Pilate asks the "Who are you?" concerning His Kingship.

(This will be discussed in the section considering the trial before Pilate).

Each of these responses is a "You said it" type of statement agreeing, "**I AM**!"

Three is the number of *certainty*. Jesus, The Christ, is the **I AM**!

But there were two more questions that obtained a response from the Lord Jesus:

(2) The Second question: Where did you come from?

(3) The Third and final question that Jesus answered: What are you going to do?

THREE TRIALS

We found three trials!!! We knew that, but had not put it all together as another confirming *triple*. We ask: "Were *three* trials necessary to emphatically *confirm* the death sentence,[93] ***Crucify Him*?**"

The (1) religious government condemned Him to death;

(2) the government of His home province condemned Him; last but not least,

(3) *Rome* the official government of the known world issued the final sentence: "***Crucify Him***."

Each trial confirmed the death sentence of a faultless man; Pilate, himself stated *thrice*: "I find no fault in him." The sentence was undeserved.

---

92   John 8:24, 28, 58.
93   The Council was "Jewish," Herod was "Ishmaelite." The Procurator was "Roman," These *three* represent the **totality** of the human race.

Yet the suffering, the sentence, and the mode of execution were all determined by God Himself.[94]

Note: Here is more great irony: Satan prompting wicked men to fulfill, to the letter,[95] God's eternal plan for the sacrificial, substitutionary, redemption of mankind. Paul clearly states: **"For he [God] hath made him [Jesus] to be sin for us, who knew no sin; that we might be made the righteousness of God in him [Jesus]"** (2 Corinthians 5:21).

The *three* epic trials of the universe were set to begin.

What were they?

Human magistrates were ready to sit as judges and condemn their Creator, the Sustainer of the universe.

They would be the judges of the One who would ultimately be their Judge!!!

Could this also be ironic?

THE TRIAL: by the *RELIGIOUS GOVERNMENT*

The first trial was religious. Amazingly, we found this to be another *triple*! The *three* religious trials take place before *three* tribunals: before Annas, before the High Priest, and finally before the Sanhedrin.

(1) Before Annas:

"Then the band and the captain and officers of the Jews took Jesus, and bound him, And led him away to Annas first; for he was father in law to Caiaphas, which was the high priest that same year. Now Caiaphas was he, which gave counsel to the Jews, that it was expedient that one man should die for the people"[96] (John 18:12-14).

(2) Before Caiaphas:

"Now Annas had sent him bound unto Caiaphas the high priest." (John 18:24)

---

[94] 1 Peter 1:20-21 "Who verily was foreordained before the foundation of the world, but was manifest in these last times for you, Who by him do believe in God, that raised him up from the dead, and gave him glory; that your faith and hope might be in God."

[95] "Till heaven and earth pass, one jot or one tittle shall in no wise pass from the law, till all be fulfilled." (Matthew 5:18)

[96] This proclamation was made in response to Lazarus being raised from the dead.

"Then took they him, and led him, and brought him into the high priest's house. And Peter followed afar off" (Luke 22:54-66).

(3) **Before the entire Council:** (The Sanhedrin)
"And as soon as it was day, the elders of the people and the chief priests and the scribes came together, and led him into their council, saying, Art thou the Christ" (Luke 22:66-67)?
"Then said they all, Art thou then the Son of God? And he said unto them, Ye say that I am.
And they said, What need we any further witness? for we ourselves have heard of his own mouth" (Luke 22:70-71).

– – – – – – – – –

Peter's denials: A well known triple is the three denials by Peter. These are recorded in each of the four gospels with each writer devoting several verses to the incident. Jesus had foretold Peter's denial; only Luke mentioned the High Priest's house. Was it at the house of the High Priest that all three denials took place? It would seem so.

Matthew 26:69-75
Mark 14: 66-72
Luke 22: 55-62
John 18:15-18; 25-27

The witness of three is a certainty, but when all four Gospels include a detailed narrative, it must have great significance.

Peter did fearfully, willfully, and deliberately deny his Lord. It is interesting to note that Peter's *three* denials were later followed by *three* repetitious questions from the resurrected Lord: "**Lovest thou me?**" "**Lovest thou me?**" "**Lovest thou me?**" (John 21:15-17)

Peter's response to each was a "Yes" to which Jesus issued *three* "work" orders: "Feed my lambs, feed my sheep, and feed my sheep."

– – – – – – – – –

Back to the trials: Jesus, in each of the three appearances before the religious rulers, proclaimed the fact that He, Himself was the promised Messiah; that He, Himself was indeed the Son of God. The religionists certainly knew what he was saying. The verdict is inevitable!

The Verdict of the Religious Trial

Jesus was pronounced as being guilty of BLASPHEMY!
The sentence: DEATH!!!

Note: Because the religionists had no authority for execution, they had to take their case to Pilate, the Roman authority for the ultimate death sentence.

THE TRIAL: by the *PROVINCIAL GOVERNMENT*

Trial two was before Herod. Trial three was before Pilate. It was only Pilate who could issue the death sentence that the religionists demanded. How did the provincial government get involved?

Immediately from the Council, Jesus was taken by the temple guard and the mob to appear before *Pilate*, the Roman procurator. Pilate made his initial interrogations and decided he wanted out of this whole scene. When he discovered that Jesus was from Galilee and that *Herod*, the provincial governor of Galilee was in town, it was an easy way out. So, Pilate sent Jesus to Herod. This is almost ironic that Pilate, the procurator of this part of the Roman world, would send Jesus to Herod, a minor provincial governor.

While it seemed that Satan was finally about to defeat God,[97] God's sovereignty is evident, even in this side issue: there needed to be *three* trials *(three witnesses)* for God's ultimate plan to stand in *certainty*, before a questioning world as an eternal testimony.

Question: Do you think it was a coincidence that Herod was in Jerusalem at this time, or was it a confirming miracle?

We look at Luke's brief account of Herod's trial:

> **Luke** 23:6-12 "And as soon as he *[Pilate]* knew that he *[Jesus]* belonged unto Herod's jurisdiction, he sent him to Herod, who himself also was at Jerusalem at that time.[98] . . . And the chief priests and scribes stood and vehemently accused him . . . . But he *[Jesus]* answered him *[Herod]* nothing."

This "trial" before Herod was brief. Jesus made no response to either Herod or to his accusers. No significant questions are recorded. Herod wanted to see a miracle, but none was performed. So Herod allowed the accusations to stand, indicating that a death sentence was okay by him.

---

[97] Jesus Christ: The Second Person of the Trinity; He is God; He is God incarnate.

[98] "When the fullness of time was come . . ." All things and all necessary people were in place for God's eternal plan to be fulfilled. Even wicked Herod was in Jerusalem at the right time to fulfill the tri-trials.

Thus, Herod also condemned Jesus to death. After mockingly presenting Jesus with one of his own royal robes,[99] he sent Jesus back to Pilate for the official summary verdict.

Therefore, in this second brief trial, Jesus was condemned and sentenced by His own Galilean governmental authority, Herod.

THE TRIAL: by the *IMPERIAL GOVERNMENT*

Now, the mob moves back to Pilate. Can we imagine Pilate's dismay as he hears and sees the clamor and the throng again milling around his court? Herod had been a coward. We can almost read Pilate's mind: "Now what can I do?" Pilate's response and the trial accounts are recorded in three Gospels:

Matthew 27:2-31

Mark 15:1-20

Luke 23:1-25 ". . . And Pilate, when he had called together the chief priests and the rulers and the people, Said unto them, . . . and, behold, I, having examined him before you, have found no fault in this man . . . No, nor yet Herod: for I sent you to him; and, lo, nothing worthy of death is done unto him . . . . But they cried, saying, Crucify him, crucify him."

Jesus was tried by the ultimate human authority of the *world*, the authority of Rome itself, by Pilate. Rome was wicked, cruel, and no doubt claimed by Satan's kingdom! Thus, it was Rome, the symbol of humanity's wicked character that would issue the *final* condemnation of the righteous King of the Jews: the King of Kings, the Lord of Lords, the Majestic, Omnipotent, Omniscient Creator and Sustainer of the universe. Satan probably smirks in confidence; he is winning his war.

Note: Jesus stood submissively, before Pilate, responding only to questions concerning His *person, mission,* and *authority.*

---

[99] "And Herod with his men of war set him at nought, and mocked him, and arrayed him in a gorgeous robe, and sent him again to Pilate." (Luke 23:11)

Section VII
Jesus Before Pilate

The Apostle, John's account of this trial includes some amazing information and numerous sets of triples. His account is teeming with evidences of God's providence as Satan and his servants ridicule *The King of the Jews,* and seemingly Satan is striking a final blow against God and His *Anointed.* However, we are about to observe an *irony* and the greatest *paradox* that history has ever known, with John punctuating the account by triples.

First, Pilate tries to identify who Jesus really is. Pilate has had years of experience in dealing with the Jewish religious leaders and even their treacherous treatment of any adversary. He is skeptical of their motives but fully aware of their jealous schemes and of their utter hatred of Rome's rule, even their hatred of Pilate himself.

Question: How many triples can you identify in the account of this trial? Are there **seven**—or are there nine?

WHO IS JESUS?

We have already looked at this, but here it is again from Pilate's viewpoint. Pilate's three questions seem to be an attempt to satisfy his curiosity, "Who are you, really?" Pilate's three questions are found in John Chapter 18, 19.

- ▶ "Art thou the King of the Jews?" (18:33)
- ▶ "What hast thou done?" (18:35)
- ▶ "Whence art thou?" (19:6)

It was interesting for us to note that Jesus spoke only to clarify His claims. He did not respond to any other questions or accusations during the three trials. He was silent throughout the extreme torture and mockery. This reaction had been predicted 700 years before by the Prophet, Isaiah: "**He was oppressed, and he was afflicted, yet he opened not his mouth: he is brought as a lamb to the slaughter, and as a sheep before her shearers is dumb, so he openeth not his mouth**" (Isaiah 53:7).

As our group studied this entire account, we found the triples to be awesomely spectacular. The theme of "Kingship" permeates the dialogue. This is what we would expect from Rome's representative.

Pilate's first recorded question: "**Art thou the King of the Jews?**"

His second, "**What hast thou done?**" brings a unique response from Jesus. "**My kingdom is not of this world; . . . , but now is my kingdom not from hence.**"

Pilate asks the final question: "**Art thou a king then?**"

Jesus responds with a definitive declaration: "**Thou sayest that I am a king. To this end was I born, and for this cause came I into the world, that I should bear witness unto the truth. Every one that is of the truth heareth my voice**" (John 18:37).

Evidently shocked by a mention of *truth*, Pilate asks, probably sarcastically, the ultimate question: "**What is truth?**"[100]

However, he does not wait for an answer from the One who had previously stated: "**I am the way, THE TRUTH, and the life**" (John 14:6).[101]

PILATE'S FINDING

Usually a judge states his sentence only once, but now we find *three* pronouncements by Pilate. Each was a "**no fault**" statement:

John 18:38 "**He went out again unto the Jews, and saith unto them, I find in him no fault at all.**"

John 19:4 "**Behold, I bring him forth to you, that ye may know that I find no fault in him.**"

John 19:6 "**Pilate saith unto them, Take ye him, and crucify him: for I find no fault in him.**"

Remember, that a thrice repeated statement is a statement of certainty. God is making thrice certain that, throughout history, all mankind will be able to read and hear the judgmental verdict concerning Jesus of Nazareth, the Christ: "**NO FAULT!**"

No Fault is stronger than a "not guilty" because a "not guilty" verdict deals only with a specific crime. Pilate's is a *triple* statement:

"**NO FAULT**"

---

[100] Was Pilate a student of Greek and Roman philosophy? Both Greek and Roman philosophers had sought answers (*truth*) but could only offer opposing arguments.

Today we have multiple points of view, often opposing each other.

Today, the question remains: "*What is Truth?*" (See http://www.3-truths.com).

However, *today* the real *answer* is still available: John 14:6; 17:17; 2 Tim. 2:15.

[101] Jesus also claimed three times to speak "*truth*" in John 8:40, 45, 46.

"**NO FAULT!'**"
"**NO FAULT!'**"

This is the most profound statement made by any human being, Jesus was/is faultless!!! He is God—He is Holy—He is faultless.

To confirm this certainty, the Holy Spirit inspired each of the three other Gospel writers to confirm this fact!

Matthew 27:24: "This just person" (27:24).

Mark 15:14 "What evil hath he done" (15:14)?

Luke 23:14-22 Luke's account also *triply* indicates Pilate's "**no fault**" pronouncement.

THE ULTIMATE IRONY

Now, back to the "kingship" theme! It was Pilate who *thrice* proclaimed Jesus as being *KING*.

But, let's become spectators at this trial. Even better, let's become *court recorders* of the proceedings. Court recorders record the words that are spoken and sometimes significant actions. They do not record either intent or attitudes.

As scribes, we have recorded a triple *kingship* question. We have recorded a triple *kingship* response. Now the ULTIMATE irony is about to be written for the annals of history.

Comment: This whole event seems inspired by an unseen realm. But we, as recorders, do not know anything of the Satanic background battle; but Satan is now prompting ridicule of Jesus claim to "Kingship."

Our Record: Let's begin our recording.

(Actually it is already recorded in Matthew 27:28-29).

"And they stripped him, and put on him

▶ a **scarlet robe**. And when they had platted

▶ a **crown** of thorns, they put it upon his head, and

▶ a **reed** in his <u>right hand</u>: and

    ◀ they **bowed** the knee

    ◀ *before* him, and mocked him,

    ◀ saying, **Hail**, King of the Jews!"

Now, review our record: what just happened? We just recorded two triples.

First, what are the *three* symbols of royalty?

▶ A *robe*,

▶ A *crown*,

▶ A *scepter*, held in the right hand.

97

Look at our record. We recorded the issuing of three symbols. We write:

A man was standing in the Roman seat of government, standing before the most senior Roman official; the man was making claims to being "A KING" and then He was presented the three royal symbols:[102] *A ROBE, A CROWN, and A SCEPTER* [rod].

Second, what else? The Roman soldiers are *bowing* as at a coronation ceremony:

- ◄ *bowing,*
- ◄ *before Him* and
- ◄ *chanting*, "Hail, King of the Jews!"

Next, we cannot help but write a puzzling question: *If they just crowned Him as a King, why are they now mocking and beating Him? This seems ironic!*

Our Record Continues: (Actually already recorded, John 19).

Pilate therefore went forth again, and saith unto them, Behold, I bring him forth to you, that ye may know that
I find no fault in him.
Then came Jesus forth, wearing the crown of thorns, and the purple robe. And Pilate saith unto them,
- ► **Behold the man!**[103]

And it was the preparation of the assover, and about the sixth hour: and he saith unto the Jews,
- ► **Behold your King**!

Question: What just happened?

Answer: Satan's servants crowned Jesus Christ as KING!!! Rome's representative, Pilate, proclaimed, **"Behold your KING."**

Question: Who is in ultimate control of this whole process?

---

[102]   *Three* symbols of Royalty: Matthew 27:28, 29—Robe, Reed, Crown; Mark 15:17—Robe, Crown: John 19:2—Crown, Robe.

[103]   This announcement was probably intended to mock both the Jews and Jesus by using the word *man*. However, it proclaims: "Behold your Messiah."

THE ULTIMATE PARADOX

Jesus is given a royal robe by Herod with a reed—the scepter of kingship. He is given a crown by the Romans, the "world" rulers.

Here Jesus stands, before Pilate; the soldiers bow and chant:

"Hail King of the Jews!"

Pilate then takes Jesus before the Jewish nation and proclaims:

"Behold your King!"

The crowning[104] of the King of kings by Satan's servants is the *ironic paradox* of all time.

God's plan from before the foundation of the world is unfolding and the *greatest VICTORY* is about to be won—the *substitutionary death* of Jesus Christ. Another paradox: Satan's best (worst) efforts to defeat God contribute to Jesus Christ's victory over sin and over Satan himself.

That is not all. It is unusual for a judge to announce a title at the trial. However, this is a different trial. It is a kangaroo court, but it is a legal court with legal proclamations.

BEHOLD YOUR KING

Now the *triple* proclamation as the response to Pilate's question: **"Art thou a king?"** Jesus responds with a question, a statement, and a "You said it," to Pilate's questions and then Pilate recognizes Jesus as King *three* times. Jesus Christ, **King**, is a *thrice trumpeted truth*. If these triples don't thrill the soul of the child of God, what will?

One: Pilate recognizes Jesus claim to being a king and makes no effort to question or refute that claim.

> **"Pilate therefore said unto him, Art thou a king then? Jesus answered, Thou sayest that <u>I am a king</u>. To this end was I born, and for this cause came I into the world, that I should bear witness unto the truth. Every one that is of the truth heareth my voice." (John 18:37)**

---

[104] We could find no other account of Jesus Christ being crowned as King. But we note: He is *thrice* proclaimed as "King of kings" in the New Testament. (1 Timothy 6:15; Revelation 17:14; Revelation 19:16).

Two: Pilate labels Jesus as "King of the Jews."

"But ye have a custom, that I should release unto you one at the passover: will ye therefore that I release unto you <u>the King of the Jews</u>?" (John 18:39)

Three: Pilate proclaims Jesus as "King."

"And it was the preparation of the passover, about the sixth hour, and he saith unto the Jews, **Behold your King!**" (John 19:14)

THE MOB'S DEMAND

The mob demands death by crucifixion. This demand was also *thrice* stated. The certainty: the mob wanted Him dead!

"When the chief priests therefore and officers saw him, they cried out, saying,

▶ **Crucify him,**

▶ **crucify him**. Pilate saith unto them, Take ye him, and crucify him: for I find no fault in him." (John 19:6)

"But they cried out, Away with him, away with him,

▶ **crucify him**. Pilate saith unto them, Shall I crucify <u>your King</u>? The chief priest answered, We have no king but Caesar." (John 19:15)

THE SENTENCE

"And it was the preparation of the passover, and about the sixth hour: and he saith unto the Jews, Behold your King! . . . Then delivered he him therefore unto them to be crucified. And they took Jesus, and led him away." (John 19:14-16)

The trial ends with no conviction but with a sentence of death. This was all in God's plan. Christ's work was foreshadowed by the Old Testament Tabernacle, by the sacrifices and feasts, and by the Levitical priesthood. His work was also foretold by the prophets, and foreordained by God the Father.

Question:

Why would God the Father plan for Jesus to suffer and die?

The answer is summarized by Jesus' own statement:

"For God so loved the world, that he gave his only begotten Son, that whosoever believeth in him should not perish, but have everlasting life.

For God sent not his Son into the world to condemn the world; but that the world through him might be saved" (John 3:16-17).

Question:

If God so loved us, wouldn't it be reasonable for the *Redeemed Ones* (us) to *trumpet* this message to those who haven't heard?

Note: The triples in the account of Jesus' suffering, trials, and sentence should thrill our hearts as we contemplate God's eternal plan and the certainty of His plan's ultimate completion. If God was so exacting to record the events as certain, shouldn't we, by faith,[105] recognize the certainty of His love, forgiveness, and provision of eternal life for all who will, by faith receive His atoning forgiveness?

Next: The *Lamb of God* died for us.

---

[105] "Jesus saith unto him, Thomas, because thou hast seen me, thou hast believed: blessed are they that have not seen, and yet have believed." (John 20:29)

Questions:

► Can you think of any triples relating to Jesus' death?
► Can you think of any triples that relate to the resurrection of Jesus Christ?
► Can you think of any triples relating to Jesus Christ's ascension into heaven?
► Can you think of any triples relating to the return of Jesus Christ?

Section VIII
The Death
Of
The Savior

As we prepared to search the events of Jesus' final 24 hours, we couldn't help but wonder, "Are there some triples in the accounts of the crucifixion?" The resounding answer was, "Yes!" We found, guess how many? How many can you find? [106] These, and their implications were absolutely awesome!

Pilate proclaimed innocence by stating "No Fault" three times and then issued the ultimate sentence by simply telling the religionists, "Here He is, you crucify Him." John records the final event:

"Then delivered he *[Pilate]* him *[Jesus]* therefore unto them to be crucified. And they took Jesus, and led him away.
And he *[Jesus]* bearing his cross went forth into a place called the place of a skull, which is called in the Hebrew Golgotha:
Where they crucified him, and two other with him, on either side one, and Jesus in the midst" (John 19:16-18).

As we looked at the actual crucifixion event, we found *nine* (9) sets of triples.

THREE CROSSES

Jesus was the center of the focus. It seems that nearly all portrayals of the crucifixion include three crosses,[107] always with Jesus on the center cross, standing higher than either of the other two. Being the highest is the artists' conjecture, but probably accurate. Jesus' cross was also the post for the proclamation of His *title* in *three* languages.

THREE MENTIONS OF SIMON

On the way to the summit of Golgotha (Calvary), Jesus fell under the weight of the cross and we find *three* mentions of Simon of Cyrene. This must be an important situation. The fact that Jesus was so weakened by the abuse is indicated by *three* Gospels. It was a visitor to Jerusalem, Simon

---

[106] Many commentators reference three mountains of Jerusalem: Zion, Moriah (the Temple mountain), and Calvary.

[107] Matthew 27:38: Mark 15:27; Luke 23:33; John 19:18

of Cyrene who was compelled to carry the heavy cross up the hill of Calvary where they crucified Jesus.

> **Matthew** 27:32 "And as they came out, they found a man of Cyrene, Simon by name: him they compelled to bear his cross."
> **Mark** 15:21
> **Luke** 23:26

It would appear that Simon, as an innocent bystander, was grabbed by a Roman soldier and compelled to carry the cross.

Note: Please allow a bit of personal speculation. Cyrene was a city in Northern Africa. It had a strong Jewish influence. My speculation is based on the assumptions that Simon was a descendent of the Hamites and also was a Jewish proselyte.

Also we note that all humankind can trace its ancestry back to Noah and his *three* sons: Shem, Ham, and Japheth. Thus all humans are descended from one of these three lines. Here is the speculation: only two lines were involved in the sentencing to death. What about the Hamites?

Then along comes an innocent bystander, grabbed by a Roman soldier and made to participate. Thus, all the descendents of Noah's *three* sons: Shem, Ham, and Japheth (*three people groups*) were represented at the death of Jesus.[108]

Interestingly, the New Testament writers who were each Jewish by birth (except Luke) and initially obedient to the Law, saw only *two* groups: Jews and Gentiles. The Scripture places them as being *equal* before God.

> "What then? are we better than they? No, in no wise: for we have before proved both Jews and Gentiles, that they are all under sin; As it is written, There is none righteous, no, not one:" (Romans 3:9-10)

Paul writes of two people groups; but for the account of Jesus' crucifixion, God may have included the third line via Simon of Cyrene. Therefore, no genetic line could say to any other, "You killed Christ!"

Paul is emphatic about the *equality* of people. He continues: "There is **none** that understandeth, there is **none** that seeketh after God. They

---

[108] The three people groups were addressed for salvation in the book of Acts:
Semitic—Jews, Acts 2:36-41,
Hamitic—Ethiopian, Acts 8:27-39,
Japhetic—Cornelius, Acts 10:1-48.

are all gone out of the way, they are together become unprofitable; there is <u>none</u> that doeth good, no, not one . . . .

There is no fear of God before their eyes. for there is no difference: . . .

For <u>all</u> have sinned, and come short of the glory of God" (Romans 3:11-23).

Note: No people group and no individual is exempted from this triple indictment. Also, there is no room for prejudice against any person or group. All are equal in God's sight and all will both individually and equally answer to Him at the judgment.[109]

THREE LANGUAGES

The title superscription: *King of the Jews* was written in *three* of the worlds utilized languages. The title is recorded by all four of the Gospel writers, with two mentioning the *three* languages.

Mathew 27:37 "This is Jesus the King of the Jews."

Luke 23:38 Three languages

John 19:19, 20 Three languages

Mark 15:26 "The King of the Jews."

John's account:

"And Pilate wrote a title, and put it on the cross. And the writing was, JESUS OF NAZARETH THE KING OF THE JEWS.

This title then read many of the Jews: for the place where Jesus was crucified was nigh to the city: and it was written in <u>Hebrew</u>, and <u>Greek</u>, and <u>Latin</u>.

Then said the chief priests of the Jews to Pilate, Write not, The King of the Jews; but that he said, I am King of the Jews.

Pilate answered, What I have written I have written" (John 19:19-22).

Why *three* languages? At that time, these three languages were the main languages of the "world." The superscription was Pilate's unintentional proclamation to the entire "world" that this man was a KING and had officially been crowned and titled as KING.

No doubt Pilate mockingly posted the *King* title, but it *was* posted as an announcement to all the world. Thus, the posting was a *thrice trumpeted*

---

[109] The only exception to a guilty finding for any individual is to have sins forgiven through faith in Jesus Christ's death, burial, and resurrection.

truth. It was a royal proclamation that is *now* being *trumpeted* throughout the world.[110]

John, as recorded in the Book of Revelation, sees Christ's second coming as the coming of the KING: "And he hath on his vesture and on his thigh a name written, KING OF KINGS, AND LORD OF LORDS" (Revelation 19:16).

THREE CRUCIFIED

Each of the four Gospels state that three persons were crucified.

Matthew 27:38 "Then were there two thieves crucified with him, one on the right hand, and another on the left."
Mark 15:27

Luke's account provides an interesting detail.

Luke 23:39-43 "And one of the malefactors which were hanged railed on him, saying, If thou be Christ, save thyself and us.
But the other answering rebuked him, saying, Dost not thou fear God, seeing thou art in the same condemnation?
And we indeed justly; for we receive the due reward of our deeds: but this man hath done nothing amiss.
And he said unto Jesus, Lord, remember me when thou comest into thy kingdom.
And Jesus said unto him, Verily I say unto thee, Today shalt thou be with me in paradise.
John 19:18

Note: Three men: One is sinless! Two are convicted sinners! One of the sinners continues his sinful rebellion against God; the other recognizes his deeds and repentantly turns to the Savior, calling Him "Lord."

These two represent all of humankind: The first, those who die not admitting their sinfulness before a Holy God.

The second thief represents those who repentantly turn to the Savior, making Him "Lord." His prayer reminds us of the publican's prayer, "**God be merciful to me a sinner**" (Luke 18:13).

---

[110] It was Jesus who said: "And this gospel of the kingdom shall be preached in all the world for a witness unto all nations; and then shall the end come" (Matthew 24:14).

Jesus responded to the thief's repentant prayer: "**And Jesus said unto him, Verily I say unto thee, To day shalt thou be with me in paradise**" (Luke 23:43).

THREE TIMES

The account of the crucifixion was divided into *three* hour time blocks.

Third Hour: Jesus was crucified the 3rd hour (Mark 15:25).

Sixth Hour: At the sixth hour began *three* hours of darkness.

Darkness from 6th hour to 9th hour (Matthew 27:45).

Darkness until the 9th hour (Luke 23:44).

Ninth Hour: At the ninth hour, Jesus died.

"Gave up the ghost" (Matthew 27:46-50).

"Gave up the ghost" (Mark 15:37).

THREE RECORDS

The awesome testimony of the Centurion's testimony is recorded by three gospel writers.

Matthew 27:54 "Truly this was the Son of God."

Mark 15:39 "Truly this man was the Son of God."

Luke 23:47 "This was a righteous man."

Note: Again allow some speculation: On the Day of Pentecost, less than two months later, ". . . **and the same day there were added unto them about three thousand souls**" (Acts 2:41).

Could it be that this centurion and/or other witnesses of Christ's death were among those first converts? Anyone present and hearing Jesus' words, "**Father forgive them, for they know not what they do**," feeling the earthquake and seeing the darkness, must have been impressed. Then on Pentecost, as they heard Peter's sermon in their own language, how could anyone avoid responding to the invitation: "**Save yourselves from this untoward generation**" (Acts 2:40)?

THREE VEIL ACCOUNTS

Three gospel writers record this event with the author of Hebrews informing us of its significance. The veil of the temple was ripped open, from top to bottom, allowing access into the Holy of Holies and to the *presence* of God. Could it be that a ministering priest witnessed this miraculous opening of the veil—the veil that symbolized man's separation from God? This significant event is mentioned by *three* of the Gospel writers.

Matthew 27:51 "And, behold, the veil of the temple was <u>rent in twain</u> from the top to the bottom; and the earth did quake, and the rocks rent;"

Mark 15:38 "And the veil of the temple was <u>rent in twain</u> from the top to the bottom."

Luke 23:45 "And the sun was darkened, and the veil of the temple was <u>rent in the midst</u>."

This was such an important symbolic event that the author of the Book of Hebrews also mentioned it three times.

Hebrews 6:19 "Which hope we have as an anchor of the soul, both sure and stedfast, and which entereth into that within the veil."

Hebrews 9:3 "And after the second veil, the tabernacle which is called the Holiest of all;"

Hebrews 10:20 "By a new and living way, which he hath consecrated for us, through the veil, ..."

Note: In the Old Testament, only the High Priest could pass the veil and enter the Holy of Holies, and then only once per year to sprinkle the blood of a lamb. Now the veil is open for all who are willing to receive Christ's redemption. We can now come by faith to God in repentance, in worship, and in petition.

THREE BURIAL ITEMS

Joseph of Arimathaea and Nicodemus used three items as they prepared Jesus' body for burial.

"And there came also Nicodemus, which at the first came to Jesus by night, and brought a mixture of myrrh and aloes, about an hundred pound weight. Then took they the body of Jesus, and wound it in linen clothes with the spices, as the manner of the Jews is to bury" (John 19:39, 40).

THREE DAYS

Jesus was truly dead. Three days in the grave. Here are three references.

Luke 24:21 "But we trusted that it had been he which should have redeemed Israel: and beside all this, to day is the third day since these things were done."

Acts 10:40 "Him God raised up the third day, and shewed him openly;"

1 Corinthians 15:4 "And that he was buried, and that he rose again the third day according to the scriptures:" [*According to the scriptures" means, according to the way the scriptures predicted He would rise*].

Note: These nine *triples* are amazing because they tell the story of redemption. Again we saw the *certainty* of the record. The clarity shows us that God intended for all who will hear His *thrice trumpeted truths* to recognize that His plan was fulfilled and was accurately recorded.

The grand finale: Jesus was in the grave *three* days. The fact that He really did die is declared as a *certainty* by the *three* days. When we state that Jesus died for me, for my sin, we know that He truly did *die*. We know that he did *pay* the penalty for the sin and sins of all will receive His gift of forgiveness and a new life in Christ.

THREE VICTORIOUS TRIUMPHS

We could begin a list of numerous triumphs—each of which can provide a victory for the child of God.

- **Victory over Satan.** Satan's effort[111] to execute Jesus Christ actually was really Jesus Christ's victory, verified by the resurrection.

- **Victory over sin.** "What shall we say then? Shall we continue in sin, that grace may abound? God forbid. How shall we, that are <u>dead to sin</u>, live any longer therein" (Romans 6:1-2)?

- **Victory over death.** "Behold, I shew you a mystery; We shall not all sleep, but we shall all be changed, In a moment, in the twinkling of an eye, at the last trump: . . .
  Death is swallowed up in <u>victory</u>" (1 Corinthians 15:51-54).

Next, we come to the most spectacular triple announcement:
"He lives"!!!

---

[111] Please allow another speculation: Satan began his rebellion with five defiant, "I will" assertions. Could it be that Charles Wesley was correct when he wrote, "Five bleeding wounds He bears, received on Calvary"? If so, the fifth wound was the piercing by the Roman spear (John 19:34). Was that fifth wound Satan's final defiant instigation against Jesus? If so—the result was the *affirmation* of Jesus *death* (Jesus really did die). Also, this final would ultimately confirmed the *reality* of His resurrection. Consequently, Jesus Christ's *resurrection* victory sealed Satan's eternal defeat. An irony!

Section IX

The Resurrection
of
Jesus Christ

Throughout the centuries there have been founders of new or revised religions. Each has died. Not one has been resurrected to life and then seen by hundreds of people. All are dead and remain dead.

However, Jesus, The Christ, the promised Messiah came to earth, born of a virgin, lived among humankind, performed miracles, proclaimed *truth* and made claims to being the *Son of God*. He was tried, found to have *no fault* but was condemned to death in each of three trials. He was crucified and buried for *three* days to prove the *certainty* of His death. He was really dead!

THREE VERIFICATIONS

Then on the First Day of the Week, the morning of the *Jewish Feast of Firstfruits*,[112] Jesus Christ showed Himself alive "by many infallible proofs."[113]

Those who saw Him were so certain of His resurrection that they were willing to lay down their lives as they proclaimed the message, "**He is risen!!!**"

Jesus rose from the dead and was seen and heard by His followers during a 40 day period before His ascension into heaven. Now, believers throughout the world are awaiting His return. "**He shall so come in like manner as ye have seen him go into heaven.**"[114]

The resurrection account is verified in so many ways by so many people that it was difficult to find any simple triples. There are numerous single statements, double statements, and many others. Whole books have

---

[112] The Feast of Firstfruits was to be celebrated on the first day of the week following Passover (Leviticus 23:5-11). That day is our Sunday, the day that we commemorate the resurrection of The Lord Jesus Christ.

[113] Acts 1:3

[114] Acts 1:11

been written on the subject of the resurrection—we were looking for triples. Yes, we found three. Are there more?

First: The Resurrection was Predicted.

The fact of the resurrection was predicted by at least *three* sources:

1. **The Old Testament** prophet's made many statements. Here is one. "Therefore my heart is glad, and my glory rejoiceth: my flesh also shall rest in hope. For thou wilt not leave my soul in hell; neither wilt thou suffer thine Holy One to see corruption." (Psalm 16:9-10)

2. **Jesus Statements** recorded by both Mark and John foretell of His death and resurrection.

   Matthew recorded *three* occasions in which Jesus predicted His resurrection.

   ▶ "From that time forth began Jesus to shew unto his disciples, how that he must go unto Jerusalem, and suffer many things of the elders and chief priests and scribes, and be killed, and <u>be raised</u> again the third day." (Matthes 16:21)

   ▶ "And they shall kill him, and the third day he shall <u>be raised</u> again. And they *[disciples]* were exceeding sorry." (Matthew 17:23)

   ▶ "Behold, we go up to Jerusalem; and the Son of man shall be betrayed unto the chief priests and unto the scribes, and they shall condemn him to death, And shall deliver him to the Gentiles to mock, and to scourge, and to crucify him: and the third day <u>he shall rise</u> again." (Matthew 20:18-19)

   Luke also records *three* statements by Jesus, declaring His resurrection.

   ▶ "Saying, The Son of man must suffer many things, and be rejected of the elders and chief priests and scribes, and be slain, and <u>be raised</u> the third day." (Luke 9:22)

   ▶ "And he said unto them, ... and the third day <u>I shall be perfected</u>." (Luke 13:32)

   ▶ "And they shall scourge him, and put him to death: and the third day he <u>shall rise again</u>. And they understood none of these things: and this saying was hid from them, neither knew they the things which were spoken." (Luke 18:33-34)

3. Witnesses' statements who had heard His claims to rise in three days. Here are three ridiculing witnesses.

▶ "And said, This fellow said, I am able to destroy the temple of God, and to build it in <u>three days</u>." (Matthew 26:61)

▶ "We heard him say, I will destroy this temple that is made with hands, and within <u>three days</u> I will build another made without hands." (Mark 14:58)

▶ ". . . the chief priests and Pharisees came together unto Pilate, Saying, Sir, we remember that that deceiver said, while he was yet alive, After <u>three days</u> I will rise again." (Matthew 27:62-63)

Second: The resurrection is recorded as an actual event.

Each of the *four* Gospels records the resurrection account.

● **Matthew** 28:5, 6 "And the angel answered and said unto the women, Fear not ye: . . . for he is risen, as he said. Come, see the place where the Lord lay."

● **Mark** 16:6 "And he saith unto them, Be not affrighted: . . . he is risen; he is not here: behold the place where they laid him."

● **Luke** 24:1-8 "Now upon the first day of the week, very early in the morning, they came unto the sepulcher, . . . And they entered in, and found not the body of the Lord Jesus.

And it came to pass, as they were much perplexed thereabout, behold, two men stood by them in shining garments: And as they were afraid, and bowed down their faces to the earth, they said unto them, Why seek ye the living among the dead?

He is not here, but is risen: remember how he spake unto you when he was yet in Galilee, Saying, The Son of man must be delivered into the hands of sinful men, and be crucified, and the third day rise again. And they remembered his words,"

● **John** 20:1-16 "The first day of the week cometh Mary Magdalene early, when it was yet dark, unto the sepulcher, and seeth the stone taken away from the sepulcher . . . .

Jesus saith unto her, Mary.

She turned herself, and saith unto him, Rabboni; which is to say, Master."

Third: Jesus rose on the Feast of Firstfruits.

Firstfruits was one of the Seven Old Testament "Feast of the Lord." On that day, Jesus appeared throughout the day to various people.

▶ ***The Morning***:

- To Mary Magdalene (John 20:11-16)
- To Simon (Luke 24:34)

Note: It is interesting that the angels first appeared to women and that Jesus first appeared to a woman. As a result it was women who were the first people to announce that Jesus was risen from the dead.

> "And returned from the sepulcher, and told all these things unto the eleven, and to all the rest. It was Mary Magdalene, and Joanna, and Mary the mother of James, and other women that were with them, which told these things unto the apostles." (Luke 24:9-10)

If the Gospels were written by "uninspired" men, none would dare to place women as proclaimers within that culture. Yet, it is God who places women in the forefront of the most significant announcement of all time.[115]

▶ ***Mid-day***: To the two disciples on the road to Emmaus

> Mark 16:12 "After that he appeared in another form unto two of them, as they walked, and went into the country."

▶ ***Night***: To the assembled disciples

> Mark 16:14 "Afterward he appeared unto the eleven as they sat at meat, and upbraided them with their unbelief and hardness of heart, because they believed not them which had seen him after he was risen."

Thus, by the end of that festival day, The Feast of Firstfruits, most of Jesus' followers had either seen Him or had heard the report, "Jesus is alive."

---

[115] The birth announcements were also made by unlikely people for that culture. It was *shepherds* that "Made known abroad," the wonderful news (Luke 2:17, 18). Also, it was a woman, *Anna* who "spake of Him to all" (Luke 2:38). The third proclaimers were the *wise men* (foreigners) who said, "We have seen His star." These men might be the expected trumpeters, but not shepherds or a woman. "But God hath chosen the foolish *[the lowly, the unexpected]* things of the world to confound the wise" (1 Corinthians 1:27).

The hymn-writer, Robert Lowry, said it clearly:
"Up from the grave he arose;
with a mighty triumph o'er his foes; . . .
He arose! He arose!
Hallelujah! Christ arose!"

Also we must note that the New Testament writers clearly proclaim the resurrection.

THREE WITNESSES

Here are three writers who boldly state that they had *seen* Jesus alive.

▶ **Peter** proclaimed: "He seeing this before spake of the resurrection of Christ, that his soul was not left in hell, neither his flesh did see corruption. This Jesus hath God raised up, whereof we all <u>are witnesses</u>. (Acts 2:31-32)

▶ **Paul** proclaimed the resurrection in the Book of Acts on *three* occasions (many more times throughout his Epistles).

- "But God raised him from the dead: . . . ." (Acts 13:30-37)
- "Whereof he hath given assurance unto all men, in that he hath raised him from the dead." (Acts 17:31)
- "That Christ should suffer, and that he should be the first that should rise from the dead, and should shew light unto the people, and to the Gentiles." (Acts 26:23)

▶ **John,** in his writings, proclaimed that he knew the living Jesus Christ.

- **John** 21:12-14 "Jesus saith unto them, Come and dine. And none of the disciples durst ask him, Who art thou? Knowing that it was the Lord. Jesus then cometh, and taketh bread, and giveth them, and fish likewise. This is now the <u>third</u> time that Jesus <u>shewed himself</u> to his disciples, after that he was risen from the dead.
- **1 John** 3:2 "Beloved, now are we the sons of God, and it doth not yet appear what we shall be: but we know that, when he shall appear, we shall be like him; for we shall <u>see him</u> as he is" *[He is alive to be seen].*
- **Revelation** 1:7 "Behold, he cometh with clouds; and every eye shall <u>see him</u>, and they also which pierced him: and all kindreds of the earth shall wail because of him. Even so, Amen."

Revelation 1:18 "I am he that liveth, and was dead; and, behold, I am alive for evermore, Amen; and have the keys of hell and of death."

ANGELIC PROCLAMATION

"He shall so come in like manner as ye have seen Him go into heaven" (Acts 1:11). These were the words spoken by the angel(s) as Jesus Christ ascended into heaven. The ascension of the Lord Jesus is a key doctrine and we searched for a triple statement related to this event. There are many references and statements but we did not find any uniquely worded triples. Did we overlook one or two or three? Whether or not this truth is trumpeted as a triple does not diminish its reality and the angelic proclamation.

Then we recalled the *three* revelatory proclamations, made by Jesus Christ Himself in the last chapter of Revelation:

"I come quickly; "I come quickly; "I come quickly."[116]

That's clear! That's definite!! That's **_CERTAIN_**!!!

The *trumpet* shall sound; Jesus Christ will return!

Questions:

▶ Will there be one trumpet or might there be three?

▶ Will there be one sound or might it be a triple sounding?

Someday we will know the answer to these questions; but we will not be focused on the trumpets nor on the sound. We will be in eternal awe of Jesus: The Christ, our Savior, our Redeemer.

He came the first time as Savior, Redeemer, Lord;

He will come the second time as the Groom, King, and Judge.

---

[116] Revelation 22:7, 12, 20

Part Four
The Gospel

Section I
Good News: Needed

Question: Why is **Good News** needed? Are there any triples that answer this question?

As the previous chapters were compiled from our searches for *thrice trumpeted truths*, we included many of our findings. One of the *trumpeted truths* is the fact that God is holy and humankind is not in harmony with God's holiness. Adam and Eve disobeyed God's command: **"Thou shalt not."** This brought the indictment against all humankind: **"There is none righteous, no not one" (Romans 3:10).**

God's entire revelation is permeated by accounts of human wickedness. God gave ten commandments to direct the nation of Israel (and all humankind) away from sin and sinning. For those who follow God's plan for successful living, He dedicated a whole passage in Deuteronomy[117] listing a score of blessings for those Israelites who were obedient.

We note that at least one grievous sin is recorded for almost all key biblical characters,[118] thus verifying the often trumpeted fact that **"All have sinned and come short of the glory of God" (Romans 3:23).**

History also testifies to the fact of human sinfulness. Only Jesus Christ was the *Sinless One*.[119]

In answer to the question: "Why is good news needed," what triples did we find? Amazingly, we found *five* sets.[120] There may be more.

---

[117] "And all these blessings shall come on thee, and overtake thee, if thou shalt hearken unto the voice of the LORD thy God" (Deuteronomy 28:2).

[118] Three exceptions could be: Joseph, Elisha, and Daniel.

[119] 2 Corinthians 5:21; Hebrews 4:15; 1 Peter 1:19.

[120] Remember Satan's *five* "I will" statements? Interesting!

(1) THE THREE ENEMIES

The first *thrice trumpeted truth* is that humankind faces *three* enemies that impact behavior: the *world*, the *flesh*, and the *devil*.

▶ **The World**: The *world* refers to the evil of the world's culture, the evil influences, and the systems of evil that are built on covetousness and lust. Both James and John speak to this point.

James 4:4 "Ye adulterers and adulteresses, know ye not that the friendship of the <u>world</u> is enmity with God? whosoever therefore will be a friend of the world is the enemy of God."

1 John 2:15 "Love not the world . . . ."

▶ **The Flesh**: Human nature's sinfulness is manifest by *fleshly sins*. Paul lists several of the *fleshly* sins.

"Now the works of the <u>flesh</u> are manifest, which are these; adultery, fornication, uncleanness, lasciviousness, idolatry, witchcraft, hatred, variance, emulations, wrath, strife, seditions, heresies, envyings, murders, drunkenness, revellings, and such like: of the which I tell you before, as I have also told you in time past, that they which do such things shall not inherit the kingdom of God." (Galatians 5:19-21)

The self-righteous Pharisees of Jesus' day felt that they were innocent of such wickedness. However, Jesus went to the heart of human wickedness in the Sermon on the Mount and they were found guilty.[121]

▶ **The Devil**: The Devil *[Satan]* and his angels are real. Satan attacked the Lord Jesus Christ with *three temptations* as recorded in Matthew 4:3-9. The Apostle Peter warns concerning Satan's activities.

"Be sober, be vigilant; because your adversary the <u>devil</u>, as a roaring lion, walketh about, seeking whom he may devour:" (1 Peter 5:8)

(2) THE PERSONAL PARADOX

The Apostle John listed *three* aspects of a fall in 1 John 2:16.

"For all that is in the world, the
▶ <u>lust of the flesh</u>, and the
▶ <u>lust of the eyes</u>, and the

---

121 "For I say unto you, That except your righteousness shall exceed the righteousness of the scribes and Pharisees, ye shall in no case enter into the kingdom of heaven." (Matthew 5:20)

▶ pride of life, is not of the Father, but is of the world."

(3) THE DOWNWARD SPIRAL

James listed *three* aspects of a downward spiral and of heart issues.

"But every man is tempted, when he is drawn away of

▶ his own lust, and enticed. Then when lust hath conceived,

▶ it bringeth forth <u>sin</u>: and sin, when it is finished,

▶ bringeth forth <u>death</u>." (James 1:14-15)

(4) THE ISSUES OF THE HEART

"But if ye have bitter envying and strife in your hearts, glory not, and lie not against the truth. This wisdom descendeth not from above, but is

▶ earthly,

▶ sensual,

▶ devilish." (James 3:14-15)

(5) THE TRIPLE INDICTMENT

Paul's statement of the equality of *all* people before God is a *triple* indictment of the human condition: "There is <u>none</u> that understandeth, there is <u>none</u> that seeketh after God. They are all gone out of the way, they are together become unprofitable; there is <u>none</u> that doeth good, no, not one" (Romans 3:11-29).

The indictment, all have gone out of God's way, is evidenced throughout history and throughout the entire human race. It becomes obvious that some good news is needed for humanity.

Question:

The next question for this study: Are there any triples that Jesus used to declare God's *good news* message?

Section II

The Good News

THE GOSPEL

There is good news—it is *The Gospel*. The gospel proclaims a redeemer who came to seek and to save that which was lost. Since all are lost, it would seem logical that each lost person would favorably respond to the possibility of being found. However, the apostle John summarized the reality: "He *[Jesus]* was in the world, and the world was made by him, and the world knew him not. He came unto his own, and his own received him <u>not</u>. But as many as received him, to them gave he power to become the sons of God, even to them that believe on his name: Which were born, not of blood, nor of the will of the flesh, nor of the will of man, but of God" (John 1:10-13).

Jesus, when speaking with Nicodemus stated a *triple* indictment. "And this is the condemnation, that light is come into the world, and men

▶ <u>loved darkness</u> rather than light, because their deeds were evil. For every one that doeth evil

▶ <u>hateth the light,</u>

▶ <u>neither cometh to the light,</u> lest his deeds should be reproved." (John 3:19-20)

The problem is three-fold: people love darkness; they hate the light; they avoid the light. Jesus stated: "I am the light of the world : he that followeth me shall not walk in darkness, but shall have the light of life" (John 8:12).

In the Old Testament, Job faced God's interrogations and repented: "Wherefore I abhor myself, and <u>repent</u> in dust and ashes" (Job 42:6).

The New Testament gospel message began with a *triple* proclamation of *repent* by John, by Jesus, and by the disciples.

▶ **John**: It was John Baptist who brought the first *repent* message. "In those days came John the Baptist, preaching in the wilderness of Judaea, And saying, <u>Repent</u> ye: for the kingdom of heaven is at hand." (Matthew 3:1-2)

▶ **Jesus**: Repent was Jesus' initial recorded message. "From that time Jesus began to preach, and to say, <u>Repent</u>: for the kingdom of heaven is at hand." (Matthew 4:17)

121

► **Disciples**: The third to proclaim the repentance requirement were the disciples. Early in His ministry, Jesus sent them out to minister. "And they went out, and preached that men should repent." (Mark 6:12)

Note: The word *repent* carries the idea of turning around; making an about-face. To *repent*, means to do a 180; to turn to God and to turn away from sin by placing faith in Jesus Christ as savior from sin. It was Jesus' death, burial, and resurrection that paid the price for my/your sin. Thus, forgiveness and a new life is available for any one who receives Christ by faith.

The Apostle Paul proclaimed the Gospel. He listed a *triple*:

"Moreover, brethren, I declare unto you the gospel which I preached unto you, which also ye have received, and wherein ye stand; By which also ye are saved, if ye keep in memory what I preached unto you, unless ye have believed in vain.

For I delivered unto you first of all that which I also received, how that

► Christ died for our sins according to the scriptures[122];
And that

► he was buried, and that

► he rose again the third day according to the scriptures:"
(1 Corinthians 15:1-4)

The phrase, "According to the scriptures," refers to the entire Old Testament message of sacrifice, substitution, and eternal life. There are scores of examples; here are three:

(1) Abraham sacrificed a lamb *in place of* Isaac.[123] This was an illustration because in the New Testament, God the Father, sacrificed THE LAMB *[Jesus Christ]* in the place of sinners.[124]

(2) The Passover required a lamb's blood to be applied to the door posts of their dwellings.[125] In the New Testament, the blood of the Lamb *[Jesus Christ]* was shed on the day of the Passover to make atonement for any who will by faith receive this atonement for their own sin (see 1 Peter 1:18-21).

---

[122] Or, [as the Scriptures said He would do].
[123] Genesis 22:13
[124] John 1:29
[125] Exodus 12:1-10

(3) The promise that the Redeemer would not see corruption (see Psalm 16:10). In the New Testament account, the Redeemer rose from the dead to be the *firstfruits* of all who believe. The Apostle Paul spoke to this truth when he wrote, "But now is Christ risen from the dead, and become the firstfruits of them that slept" (1 Corinthians 15:20).

"He is not here: for he is risen, as he said. Come, see the place where the Lord lay." (Matthew 28:6)

THE MESSAGE

The message is simple: Jesus Christ paid the penalty for our sin. He died because of our sin. He was our substitute. He died in my/your place. Because of Christ's death, burial and resurrection, we can now come to God because the veil was opened when Jesus stated: "It is finished." This truth of redemption and also of access to God was promised and then proclaimed by the prophets and, most importantly by God Himself as Father, Son and Holy Spirit.

► **God**: Old Testament:

"Wash you, make you clean; put away the evil of your doings from before mine eyes; cease to do evil; . . .

Come now, and let us reason together, saith the LORD: though your sins be as scarlet, they shall be as white as snow; though they be red like crimson, they shall be as wool." (Isaiah 1:16-18)

► **Jesus Christ**:

"Come unto me, all ye that labour and are heavy laden, and I will give you rest." (Matthew 11:28)

► **The Holy Spirit and Jesus Christ**: (A *triple* invitation)

"And the Spirit and the bride say, Come. And let him that heareth say, Come. And let him that is athirst come. And whosoever will, let him take the water of life freely." (Revelation 22:17)

THE INVITATION

The invitation is simple. It is a simple *come by faith* invitation. Here are three proclamations:

► Jesus stated the simple invitation:

"Come unto me" (Matthew 11:28-30).

► Turn from sin. Paul summarized his message with these words:

". . . that they should repent and <u>turn</u> to God, and do works meet for repentance" (Acts 26:20).

► God will forgive sin:

"In whom we have redemption through his blood, the forgiveness of sins, according to the riches of his grace" (Ephesians 1:7).

THE BOOK OF LIFE

We found eight references to the *Book of Life* in the New Testament, so that is not a triple. Here is the most definitive passage.

"And I saw the dead, small and great, stand before God; and the books were opened: and another book was opened, which is the book of life : and the dead were judged out of those things which were written in the books[126], according to their works.

And the sea gave up the dead which were in it; and death and hell delivered up the dead which were in them: and they were judged every man according to their works.

And death and hell were cast into the lake of fire. This is the second death. And whosoever was not found written in <u>the book of life</u> was cast into the lake of fire." (Revelation 20:12-15)

This and other passages tell us that those whose names are NOT found in the *Book of Life* will not enter heaven (Rev. 21:27; Phil. 4:3).

Questions:

► **Is your name written in the Book of Life?**

With this question, please allow me to speak personally to anyone who has not received forgiveness and a new life in Christ.

God is RIGHTEOUS; God is HOLY. It is impossible for any person to measure up to God's RIGHTEOUSNESS. God has said concerning all people: "There is none righteous, no not one" and "For all have sinned and come short of the glory of God" (Romans 3:10, 23).

The Gospel is God's *Good News*. Jesus clearly states the *for whom* and *the why* He came. Jesus said: "For the Son of man is come to seek and to save that which was lost" (Luke 19:10).

"I am come that they might have life, and that they might have it more abundantly" (John 10:10).

---

[126] "<u>The books</u>" refers to "books of record," not the Book of Life.

Jesus Christ died to provide a free gift of forgiveness, righteousness and eternal life to any who will receive Him by turning to God and by faith receive this free gift.

Jesus not only died but He rose from the dead and now lives to provide this new life for any person who will by faith, receive His gift. By faith, the gift of forgiveness and of a new life can be yours.

▶ **What is the *New Birth?***

There are three significant descriptions of God's work in the human heart: the *new birth, imputed righteousness,* and a *new life.* These are the gifts of God as stated in Ephesians 2. These *three works* of God are only separated by their descriptive illustrations, not by time.

It was Jesus who spoke of the new birth when He said, "**Ye must be born again.**" The term *"born again"* is used exactly *three* times in the New Testament. Jesus introduced it by a double usage in His dialogue with Nicodemus and Peter used it one time in his first epistle.

John 3:3 "Jesus answered and said unto him, Verily, verily, I say unto thee, Except a man be

▶ **born again**, he cannot see the kingdom of God" (John 3:3).

John 3:7 "Marvel not that I said unto thee, Ye must be

▶ **born again.**"

1 Peter 1:23 "Being

▶ **born again**, not of corruptible seed, but of incorruptible, by the word of God, which liveth and abideth for ever" (1 Peter 1:23)

We also looked at Jesus' *born again* requirement in John's gospel, then we found that John had already recorded the source of this *birth* event.

"But as many as <u>received him</u>, to them gave he power to become the <u>sons of God</u>, even to them that <u>believe</u> on his name: Which were **born**, not of blood, nor of the will of the flesh, nor of the will of man, but <u>of God</u>." (John 1:12-13)

Then we turned to the book of First John. Amazingly we found the term *"born of God" **seven*** times[127] if we begin with the *"born of him"* in chapter two. If three declares certainty, *seven* must be a *definite* certainty. God is saying—attention please! Being *born again* is the key element for a new life in Christ.[128]

---

[127]   (1 John 2:29; 3:9, 9; 4:7; 5:1, 4, 18).

[128]   See also Galatians 3:6.

Just as with a human birth—the one being born is the one acted upon, not the actor. The new birth is *of God*. God does the regenerating work. What we do or what someone else does for us or to us is not this birth process. It is God that forgives our sin; He *births* us into the family of God, and imparts a *new life* through Christ. It is then *His Robes for Mine*.[129] I allow Him to take *my* robes of sinfulness and He gives me *His* robe of righteousness.

IMPUTED RIGHTEOUSNESS

This switching of "robes" is known as *imputation*. The example of Abraham's *belief* and God viewing him as righteous is cited three times.

- ▶ "And he believed in the LORD; and he <u>counted it</u> to him for righteousness." (Gen 15:6)
- ▶ "For what saith the scripture? Abraham believed God, and it was counted unto him for righteousness." (Rom 4:3) "And therefore it was <u>imputed</u> to him for righteousness." (Rom 4:22)
- ▶ "And the scripture was fulfilled which saith, Abraham believed God, and it was <u>imputed</u> unto him for righteousness: and he was called the Friend of God." (James 2:23)

How can this be? God said concerning Jesus and His death, "**For he hath made him *[Jesus Christ]* to be sin for us, who knew no sin; that we might <u>be made</u> the righteousness of God in him**" (2 Corinthians 5:21).

Because of Jesus' sinless life and of His death for us, God will both grant to us **forgiveness** of sin and ***impart*** *righteousness* (endow us with Christ's righteousness). The price Jesus paid was great but for us the process is simple.

Jesus said, *"repent"* (Matthew 4:17). To *repent*, means to do a 180; *to turn to God*, away from sin, by faith *[trust]* in Jesus Christ, asking God's forgiveness for your sin. God will forgive because of what Jesus Christ has done for you on the cross.

By faith, trust in Jesus Christ, you will be given Christ's righteousness[130] and eternal life. Your name will be written in *The Book of Life*. Do this and receive God's promise: "**As many as <u>received him</u> *[Jesus Christ]*,**

---

[129] http://www.churchworksmedia.com/hymns/his-robes-for-mine-text/
[130] http://www.churchworksmedia.com/hymns/his-robes-for-mine-text/

to them gave he power to become the sons of God, even to them that believe on his name" (John 1:12).

What a person does with Jesus Christ is the most important decision that can ever be made; this decision determines our eternal destiny.

NEW LIFE

No study of The Gospel can be complete without finding a triple reference to this *new life* in Christ.

> ► "Therefore if any man be in Christ, he is a <u>new</u> creature: old things are <u>passed away</u>; behold, all things are become <u>new</u>. And all things are of God, who hath reconciled us to himself by Jesus Christ, and hath given to us the ministry of reconciliation." (2 Corinthians 5:17-18)

Two other passages speak of the newness of life.

> ► Ephesians 4:24-25 "And that ye put on the <u>new</u> man, which after God is created in righteousness and true holiness. Wherefore putting away lying, speak every man truth with his neighbour: for we are members one of another."

> ► Colossians 3:8-10 "But now ye also put off all these; anger, wrath, malice, blasphemy, filthy communication out of your mouth. Lie not one to another, seeing that ye have put off the old man with his deeds; And have put on the <u>new</u> man, which is renewed in knowledge after the image of him that created him:"

NEW LIFE-STYLE

The new life results in *new attitudes* toward God, His Word, and God's children. Here are three of the seven passages in 1 John indicating that being born of God produces new attitudes.

> ► "If ye know that he is righteous, ye know that every one that doeth righteousness is born of him." (1 John 2:29)

> ► "Whosoever believeth that Jesus is the Christ is born of God: and every one that loveth him that begat loveth him also that is begotten of him." (1 John 5:1)

> ► "Beloved, let us love one another: for love is of God; and every one that loveth is born of God, and knoweth God" (1 John 4:7).

This new life also results in new power, through the working of God's Holy Spirit in the newly born *child of God*. Paul speaks to this point: "For it

is God which worketh in you both to will and to do of his good pleasure"
(Philippians 2:13).

To be *born again* obviously means to be *born of God*. It is this new birth
that places the redeemed person as a *child of God* into the *family of God* with
a *new life*.

Questions:

▶ What do you think might be the greatest miracle of God's grace?
▶ After reading the above triples, could you show a person how to
receive forgiveness of sin and be born again into the family of God?
▶ Are there any other New Testament passages that speak of this *new
life?*

Section III
The Return of Jesus Christ

The return of Jesus Christ is a major theme throughout the Scriptures. Associated with this event is the sounding of *The Trumpet of God*. You may not believe it, but we found *three* and only *three* New Testament passages that *trumpet the truth* for the Trumpet's sounding at the return of Christ.

THE TRUMPET SOUND

- **Matthew** 24:31 "And he shall send his angels with a great sound of a <u>trumpet</u>, and they shall gather together his elect from the four winds, from one end of heaven to the other."
- **1 Corinthians** 15:52 "In a moment, in the twinkling of an eye, at the last trump: for the <u>trumpet</u> shall sound, and the dead shall be raised incorruptible, and we shall be changed."
- **1 Thessalonians** 4:16-18 "For the Lord himself shall descend from heaven with a shout, with the voice of the archangel, and with the <u>trump</u> of God: and the dead in Christ shall rise first:

   Then we which are alive and remain shall be caught up together with them in the clouds, to meet the Lord in the air: and so shall we ever be with the Lord.

   Wherefore comfort one another with these words."

While there is general agreement that the *trumpet* signals the END TIME events, there are at least three major views concerning the specific meaning of the *trumpet sounding*.

- The *trumpet sounding* will mark the *end* of the world.
- The *trumpet sounding* will signal the *rapture* of all living believers and the resurrection of all believers who have died.
- The *trumpet sounding* will begin the *judgment* of this world system.

As we considered these and other passages, we were convinced that this sounding will announce the *rapture [catching away]* of all believers with this description being vividly described by the previously listed passage from 1 Thessalonians 4:16-18.

While there are differences of opinion as the specific sequence of end-time events, we can be certain that the *trumpet* will sound and ***God's eternal plan will be implemented***.

God planned Christ's first coming, with His purpose and plan being perfectly executed. We can be certain that His complete purpose and plan will again be perfectly executed at the sounding of *The Trump of God*.

Question:

► When will Jesus Christ return?

Answer: Jesus came to earth the first time at the **right time** as stated by the Apostle Paul: "But when the <u>fulness of the time</u> was come, God sent forth his Son" (Galatians 4:4).

His second coming will also be at **the right time**.

The return of the Lord Jesus Christ is *imminent*.[131] *Imminent* means that His return could be *at any moment*.[132]

Our responsibility: be ready!

THE FINAL PROMISE

Here we are at the Scripture's final *thrice trumpeted truth*. This *concluding triple* was spoken by Jesus Christ Himself. This is a spectacular *triple* proclamation of *certainty*.

"Behold,

► **I come quickly**: blessed is he that keepeth the sayings of the prophecy of this book . . . .

And, behold,

► **I come quickly**; and my reward is with me, to give every man according as his work shall be . . . .

He which testifieth these things saith, Surely

► **I come quickly**. Amen." (Revelation 22:7-20)

This spectacular *triple* in the final Chapter of God's revelation becomes the final announcement. It is a *certain* promise of an *imminent* event.

---

131 *Imminent*: Jesus Christ may come in the next moment or He may come later. We do not know when. Many scholars believe it will be during the two day Feast of Trumpets, *Rosh Hashanah*. It could be either of the two days??? Any who have tried, or will try to set a date will look foolish and great ridicule and embarrassment will result.

132 There are *three* events in the life of each individual that are *imminent*: death, the return of Christ, and judgment.

Conclusion:

Three thousand years ago, Solomon penned a timeless conclusion when he wrote: "Let us hear the conclusion of the whole matter: Fear God, and keep his commandments: for this is the whole duty of man. For God shall bring every work into judgment, with every secret thing, whether it be good, or whether it be evil" (Ecclesiastes12:13-14).

Our conclusion:
Christ's coming is *imminent*!
It will be spectacular!
It is ***certain***!

John adds two final prayers:
Even so, come, Lord Jesus.
The grace of our Lord Jesus Christ be with you all. Amen"
(Revelation 22:20, 21).

For more notes on triple truths
see
http//www.3-truths.com

Appendix A
Repetition in Genesis 6, 7, 8

Why a Flood?

The earth also was <u>corrupt</u>   (Genesis 6:11)

The earth was filled with *violence*   (6:11)

It was <u>corrupt</u>   (6:12)

For all flesh had <u>corrupted</u> his way   (6:12)

The earth is filled with *violence*   (6:13)

I will destroy man   (6:7)

I will destroy them   (6:13)

I, even I, do bring a flood of waters

upon the earth, to destroy all flesh   (6:17)

Who was saved?

But <u>Noah</u> found grace in the eyes

of the Lord   (6:8)

<u>Noah</u> was a just man . . .

and <u>Noah</u> walked with God   (6:9)

Thee *[Noah]* have I seen

righteousness before me   (7:1)

Thou *[Noah]* and thy sons, and

thy wife, and thy sons' wives   (6:18)

His *[Noah's]* sons, and his wife,

and his sons wives   (7:7)

The sons of Noah, Noah's wife,

and the three wives of his sons   (7:13)

thou *[Noah]*, and thy wife, and thy sons, and

thy sons' wives   (8:16)

[***Note:*** *Noah walked with God and*

he was viewed as being righteous.]

Those saved: (Eight persons)

And Noah *[1]* went forth, and

his sons *[3]*, and

his wife *[1]*, and

his sons' wives *[3]* with him   (8:18)

Criteria for death: (Stated three times)

Wherein is the <u>breath of life</u>   (6:17)

Wherein is the <u>breath of life</u>   (7:15)

All in whose nostrils was

the <u>breath of life</u>   (7:22)

Reproduction was planned:

Two of every sort   (6:19)

Two of every sort   (6:20)

Not clean, by two   (7:2)

Two and two of all flesh   (7:15)

Clean beast by sevens   (7:2)

Male and female   (6:19)

Male and his female   (7:2)

Male and the female   (7:3)

Male and the female   (7:9)

Male and female   (7:16)

After his kind   (7:14)

After their kind   (7:14)

After his kind   (7:14)

After his kind   (7:14)

That they may breed abundantly . . .

Be fruitful, multiply   (8:17)

fruitful, multiply, replenish   (9:1)

Which animals?

<u>Clean</u> beasts

beasts that are <u>not clean</u>, and of

fowls, and everything

that creepeth upon the earth   (7:8)

And every fowl after his kind and every

bird of every sort   (7:14)

Both the

fowl and of

cattle, and of

beasts, and of

every creeping thing that creepeth

upon the earth and every MAN   (7:21)

Bring forth with thee every living thing . . . ,

    of all flesh, both of fowl,

    and of cattle, of every creeping

    thing that creepeth   (8:17)

Every beast,

    every creeping thing, and every fowl, and

    whatsoever creepeth upon the earth,

    after their kinds went forth . . .   (8:19)

Time clarity:

Seven days   (7:4)

Seven days   (7:10)

Second month, 17th day of the month (7:11)

Forty days and forty nights   (7:4)

Forty days and forty nights   (7:12)

Forty days upon the earth   (7:17)

One hundred and fifty days   (7:24)

Ark rested in the seventh month   (8:4)

Seventeenth day of the month   (8:4)

At the end of 40 days,

    Noah opened the window   (8:6)

Second month on the

    seven and twentieth day   (8:14)

Water depth:

Waters increased   (7:17)

Waters increased   (7:18)

Waters prevailed   (7:18)

Prevailed exceedingly   (7:19)

Waters prevailed   (7:20)

Waters prevailed   (7:24)

Water covered!

High Hills—under the

    whole heaven, were covered   (7:19)

Mountains covered   (7:20)

Waters were on

    the face of the whole earth   (8:9)

Water dried up!

Waters returned   (8:3)

Waters were abated   (8:3)

Waters decreased   (8:5)

Waters were dried up   (8:7)

Noah knew that

    the waters were abated   (8:11)

The earth dried   (8:14)

Note: Repetition is a key for clarity—*certainty.*

CPSIA information can be obtained at www.ICGtesting.com
Printed in the USA
LVOW05s0407010514

383875LV00002B/3/P